Artists Handbooks 5
Organising Your Exhibition

The self-help guide

by **Debbie Duffin**

AN
PUBLICATIONS

Artists Handbooks

Artists Handbook 5: Organising Your Exhibition – The self-help guide is one of a series of source books which builds into a compendium of practical advice to help artists and makers operate as professionals. See pages 112 – 114 for details of other Artists Handbooks and other AN Publications.

The Author Debbie Duffin is an artist and lecturer in art education. She has extensive experience in exhibiting and writes, lectures and holds workshops on professional skills for artists.

Author's dedication This book is dedicated to my father, Dr. W. J. Duffin

First edition The first edition of this book, edited by Jonathan Harvey, was published under the title of 'Organising Your Own Exhibition: A Guide for Artists' in 1987 by ACME Housing Association Ltd, ISBN 0 950692 32 8

Production **Sub-Editor** Sharon McKee
Index & Further Information compiled by Caroline Lambert

Design & Production Richard Padwick & Neil Southern
Printed Mayfair Printers, Print House, William Street, Sunderland, SR1 1UI
Copyright **Debbie Duffin** © 1987, 1991
Publication AN Publications (Artic Producers Publishing Co Ltd) © 1991

ISBN **Second edition** 0 907730 14 0

AN Publications is an imprint of
Artic Producers Publishing Co Ltd
PO Box 23, Sunderland SR4 6DG tel 091 567 3589

Contents

Contents

1 • Introduction

Opportunities for artists to show their work severely decreased during the '70s and early '80s and although interest seemed to grow during the eighties, the current recession, which is badly affecting many galleries, means it is once again becoming more difficult for artists to find opportunities. For some the first chance never seems to come, for others it is increasingly difficult to show either as often as they would like or in the way they would like. As a result many who turned to organising their own exhibitions early in their careers, are still finding this is a useful supplement. For younger artists organising shows, even as students, it is becoming the accepted thing to do.

Many artists are taking part in a vastly growing network of 'alternative events' often aimed at a wider audience and without the restrictions imposed by an established gallery or organisation. Artists are also finding it satisfying to collaborate with the establishment in a wide range of exciting ways. All these events are now looked on as making a substantial contribution to the art world.

Since 1987 this book has become an essential aid to a growing number of artists. In spite of the revolution in the ways artists show their work, many still leave their education with little practical knowledge of the mechanics of organising shows. As an artist myself and while working with many others it has become obvious that many find it difficult to know where to turn for support, information and advice.

This handbook is still the major source on the subject, and is intended to provide practical advice on all aspects of exhibition organising, especially for those showing in this way for the first time. I have tried to cover a wide range of possibilities and to explain the most usual procedures as well as suggest alternatives, in a clear and detailed way relevant to artists. This handbook is intended to act as a guide, not a rule book, and I hope artists will select what is important and relevant to their work and personal approach. Artists will have ideas of their own and an imaginative idea may help attract attention to an artists work. I hope this book will help artists present their ideas in the best possible way and think about the relationship between what they do and what happens for them.

I have tried to include as much information and useful tips as I can, based on my own experience and with advice from many others. In particular I would like to thank Antonia Dewhurst, John Gibson and Deanna Petherbridge for their advice and help. I have received many words of support from those who have used this publication to successfully organise exhibitions for themselves; if you have any suggestions to make or useful hints to add, I would be happy to hear from you.

2 • Why organise your own exhibition

Organising your own exhibition involves a considerable amount of time, energy, and possibly money (though how much will vary with your approach). So why do it? Ideally most artists would be happy to exhibit regularly in spaces which show their work at its best, with supportive gallery directors to promote and sell their work. In practice, few find themselves in such an ideal situation. Many find they are unable to show at all within the established sector of the art world and some do not wish to show with existing galleries and prefer to have control over their own career.

It can be particularly difficult to persuade someone to show your work if you have not shown before. Some galleries like to see a track record before they will consider you for an exhibition. It may be that your work is not easy to put across through documentation, or it might be difficult to find the kind of space you need. Many galleries specialise in particular kinds of work, or take a particular approach to their exhibitions, and many only show artists by invitation. If they don't know your work, you won't be considered.

It may sound difficult to overcome such barriers, but simply working away in your studio waiting for the right opportunity to come along is unlikely to alter the situation. You can begin to change things by organising your own exhibition. This draws attention to your work and can open up other opportunities for you.

Your first exhibition can be the hardest to achieve but by providing this for yourself you are over the first hurdle. You want the experience to be a good one, a valuable contribution to your life as an artist, and you want to make the most of it by knowing how to reach your audience and how best to present your work.

There are many advantages in organising your own exhibition. First of all, you are not subject to the selection procedures of others; you are free to show your work in a way with which you feel happy. You have considerable control, all decisions are yours, you can make sure things are done properly, and set the atmosphere of your exhibition. If you sell work you probably don't have to pay commission. At the same time you are gaining valuable experience and publicity which can work for you in the future.

If, at a later date, you are offered the opportunity to show elsewhere, where you have less control, it is always useful to have a good idea of what is involved and to understand the effects on your audience of what you do. I have known artists who have exhibited in established venues, with experienced staff, to be disappointed with the results, due to a simple oversight by the gallery, for example, invitations being sent out too late.

If you know what is involved, you are far better equipped to spot when something is wrong, and ask for what you want.

To see your work in a different environment helps you to be more objective and to move on afterwards. The experience in organisation, in coping with difficulties, and dealing with people can lead to greater confidence in approaching galleries.

Finally, although you do have considerable freedom, do recognise you may not be the most objective when dealing with your own work. Enlist the help of others wherever possible.

3 • First questions to ask yourself

When to show?

You will need to ask yourself how you feel about your work being made public. Will your work be ready? Will it be seen at its best at this time? Will you want to be remembered for the work you are making now? Have you allowed enough time to organise the show as well as make the work?

On the other hand, you might feel that showing your work is an integral part of what you do as an artist, and that it may be seen at any stage in its development. Assess whether an exhibition at this time will be a good experience for you. Consider the time of year you choose, in relation to where you intend showing and to who your audience might be.

For example, summer may be a bad time as many people are away. This will apply especially if the town or city revolves around a college or university. These shut down for up to three months in summer. On the other hand, if tourists might make up the majority of your potential audience, summer could be a good time. Perhaps some big local event goes on at one time in the year and your audience, and the possibility of sales, might go up considerably if you hold your exhibition then. You might even consider investigating the possibility of 'plugging-in' to existing local events such as a festival or arts event. Contact the local council's Arts and Entertainments Department (or Leisure and Recreation Services) or the local Tourist Information Centre, to find out what is going on in the area. It's worth spending a little time on local research, if you have a choice of when and where you show.

Alone or with others?

Going it alone does, of course, give you considerable freedom; all choices and decisions are yours, you may have more space to show your work and there are no conflicts with others. But you will have to shoulder all the work and responsibility, and bear all the costs. In addition, you may need practical help, and you may find you have to pay for it.

Exhibiting with others does have many advantages. Costs, work and invigilation are shared. There is access to a greater variety of skills, experience and contacts. You may find the public takes a greater interest in a group event, and it is easier to approach people for support. You also have mutual support and back-up.

Showing in a group has other benefits. It is a good way of widening your own audience. Each artist involved will already have their own invited audience, so the number of people is multiplied; you never know when a visitor invited by someone else will become interested in your work. Generally, a group exhibition can be much more profitable in many ways for a very small outlay from each artist.

However, there are difficulties which can arise in working within a group. Remember everyone will be under pressure and this can lead to frayed tempers. It is a lot of work, and many artists will be involved in other things at the same time. Each artist will feel his or her own work is important, each will have an idea of what they want, and about how things should be done. Some time will need to be spent deciding how things will be done, how time is organised, how work and responsibilities are shared. Simple things, like someone forgetting to do what they promised, or not turning up at an agreed time, can lead to arguments.

So consider carefully who you exhibit with. Things will work out better if you know each other well for one or two people to be 'put in charge', with others willing to help when needed.

If you are involved in a large event, you will need to elect a small committee to organise the work, perhaps three or four people who have the time and interest to put into it. You might even decide to bring in an outside administrator to organise the event, or a fundraiser who would raise funds, while you, the artists, deal with the organisation.

If you do decide to work with an outside administrator, you will still need to elect an organising committee to liaise between the group and the administrator. This means decisions will be made by the committee on behalf of the artists, which will then be communicated to the administrator.

First of all you, the artists, will need to decide what part of the organising you will take on and what you would like an administrator to do. Elect your committee who can then set about finding a suitable administrator. Begin by asking other artists, artists' groups and possibly galleries, to see if anybody can recommend someone. You can advertise in specialist art publications, national newspapers and, in London, in such publications as Time Out and City Limits. When considering who to take on, check out their previous work record. If possible contact someone for whom they have worked before.

Once you have chosen your administrator, sit down with him or her, and make sure that everyone is clear about who is responsible for what. Put this in writing as an agreement between the artists and the administrator. List the artists' responsibilities, which are undertaken by the committee, and the administrator's responsibilities. Two copies of this should be made, and signed by one of the committee and by the administrator. This can then be referred to if there are any disputes.

The committee will need to maintain regular contact with the administrator and the artists in the group. For this type of event it is likely that large sums of money will be involved. The committee will need to elect one person to act as treasurer, preferably someone with some experience, or at least someone who feels confident they can keep accounts and deal with sums of money to the exact penny. The committee will also need to open a bank account in the name of the artists' group, and two committee members as signatories. Cheques can then only be issued with both signatures. The treasurer keeps the cheque book and fills out details of each cheque on the stub as with any bank account. This is particularly important when organising a large event, involving many small sums. Every transaction should be itemised in an account book.

Every group event will, of course, be different. But whenever you are working with others, it is important from the outset that it is clear who is responsible for what.

Expectations

Do you see it simply as a way to re-assess your work, of getting it out of the studio? Or as a way of gaining useful experience for the future? Do you hope it will add to your reputation as an artist? Are you hoping to gain other opportunities; in which case who will your publicity be aimed at? Is it a way of communicating with a local audience, or do your ambitions lie further afield? Is your main aim to sell work, or are you more concerned with showing larger or unsaleable work? Is this perhaps the best way to present an installation or a performance piece?

Make sure your aims are realistic. If this is your first exhibition, don't expect or take on too much. You may need to see this first experience as a way of learning and re-assessing yourself for what lies afterwards; you probably won't achieve your wildest dreams. Take things a step at a time.

4 • Finding exhibition space

Regional arts boards

see 16 • Contacts Your regional arts board (as the regional arts associations in England are now called), the Welsh regional arts associations, the Scottish Arts Council or the Arts Council of Northern Ireland should have a list of spaces available for hire within the area and lists of public places which mount exhibitions. They may be able to help with other types of spaces, by putting you in touch with someone else.

Self-organising galleries

These galleries vary greatly in size, character, cost, location and what they provide, so phone around for details. If your regional arts board can't see 17 • Further Reading provide you with a list of these, the 'Directory of Exhibition Spaces' published by AN Publications, should help.

When you have basic details, select a few which sound interesting and follow up with a visit when an exhibition is on. If you can, talk to the artists. Listen to their experiences, and note any mistakes they've made or problems they've had. But don't be put off if their feeling is negative. Remember, what you get out of your exhibition will depend on what you put in.

Colleges and polytechnics

These also vary greatly, so find out the policy of each individual institution. Some have finance and provide assistance, but others have no money available. Some will leave you more or less to yourself, others want more control. The nature of the spaces will vary too, from screens in a corridor to specially converted exhibition halls. The Directory of Exhibition Spaces also lists this type of venue.

Restaurants, theatres and...

These types of spaces will usually only suit two-dimensional and smaller works. Remember their primary purpose is their trade; your work will be seen as secondary. Those in charge may have little or no knowledge of contemporary art, and little idea of your needs.

However, you do have a guaranteed audience, a good possibility of sales at very little financial outlay and, venues of this kind are often willing to take work without charge; some might even help with expenses, especially in kind. For example, a restaurant might provide food and drink for a private view.

Your local council

Most councils have an arts and recreation department, and a budget for the arts. In some councils this is the responsibility of the libraries department. Libraries are supposed to have a space where exhibitions can be mounted. Some can also provide a list of available local venues (although this may not be very comprehensive). Remember public places which are not geared to showing artists' work may view your exhibition very differently from the way you do. Some libraries have picture loan schemes which enable people to borrow original art works for a limited period of time and a small charge. If the library finds visitors take an interest in your work, it will be an added bonus if they include some of your work in such a scheme.

If the space offered by libraries is not really suitable for you, the arts and recreation department may be able to suggest other more suitable local venues. If not, you could try the property department of your local council. Ask what kind of empty properties they have and if they can send you a list. Or try it the other way round – look around your area for an empty building that suits your needs, then contact the local rates department to find out if it is council or privately owned. If it is council owned you can make further enquiries, if it is privately owned, they will not be able to tell you who the owner is, but they might be able to pass a letter on to the owner.

see 'Using empty
spaces', below

Remember, if you take on an empty building there may be a lot of work to do, but you will probably have relative freedom to do as you please. You could also come up with a large space in this way.

Estate agents

This is probably the most difficult way to get hold of a space. Many estate agents will not be interested in your ideas, but they should be able to provide you with a list of spaces available through them. However, rents are likely to be commercial. If the estate agent is sympathetic, this can be useful in terms of being able to use a space on a short term basis. He might even agree to negotiate with the owner on your behalf. Obtaining space in this way can be very rewarding. You will have freedom in what you are able to do. There are some very beautiful and large empty buildings about which will make excellent temporary exhibition spaces.

Advertise in property sections of local papers

This may not yield results, but if someone does answer your advertisement, it can save you a lot of time and effort in searching or persuading someone to let you use a space.

Your home or studio

In many ways this is the easiest way of showing your work. It cuts out looking for a space and dealing with other people, and costs nothing in rental.

However, your home or studio may not be readily accessible to your audience, and you miss out on the experience of approaching and working with others, which can give valuable insights for the future. It can also be of great benefit to your work, to see it outside your own territory. So there are things to be gained in being a little more adventurous which can help increase your confidence.

Miscellaneous

There are many other places which might be used to exhibit your work. I have known artists set up shows in churches, museums, launderettes, hospitals, shops, municipal buildings, gardens, parks, art fairs, trade fairs, hotels, swimming pools, sports centres. The list is endless. The main thing is to look for a space which will suit your work and your aims. At the same time bear in mind the principal use of the venue and the needs and wishes of those involved. Make sure you take these into account when first approaching them.

Using empty spaces

If you are considering using an empty space, especially one which has been empty for some time, there are several points to think about.

Taking on such a space can involve considerable work. Begin by asking yourself how suited the space is to your needs and what you might have to do to bring it up to your requirements. It must be good enough to show your work to advantage, and it must be safe. For example, check the electrical installation is in good working order and that the building is secure from intruders.

Spaces which have been empty for some time may well be best suited to those who work with installation, multi-media or performance, where the raw nature of the space can not only be tolerated, but worked with or used to advantage, so little time and effort is needed.

Turning such a space into a conventional gallery may well be worth doing if you are part of a group, or if you know other artists who might want to use the space after you. A space can gradually be transformed over a period of time, so that the way it is used will change as it is transformed. The first few shows could suit the space as it is, each artist or group making their contribution to its development, so later exhibitions can be those which require a more conventional space.

Approaching people

If you intend approaching an individual or organisation to use their property or venue temporarily, start by doing some research on the organisation, the individual and the area. Find out who you will be dealing with, what their position is, what their concerns are and what their political stance might be. Try to see your approach from their point of view and what benefits you might be able to offer them, how you might convince them and what they might see as disadvantages.

Have a clear idea of what you want to do, how much time you need, some idea of the costs involved and how much you are prepared to spend.

Draft a simple proposal. Write a letter to accompany this explaining your ideas and suggesting what benefits might be derived. Suggest a meeting to discuss the idea.

Follow this up with a phone call ten to fourteen days later. Make sure you speak to the person concerned. You will have far more chance of being able to use a space if you are able to meet the person involved. They will begin to see you as an individual, and if they become sympathetic this may help.

Be prepared to take some time, those concerned may need persuading, and for eventual rejection. To many property owners this will be a new idea and they may take some convincing. If you have no luck the first time, try at least to gain some idea of what their objections are to provide useful hints for future approaches.

Do persevere. Artists have found, and very successfully used, many and varied venues to exhibit their work.

5 • Finance

Possible Exhibition Expenses

		£
Venue Costs	rent	_____
	rates	_____
	electricity	_____
	heating	_____
	building insurance	_____
Publicity	invitation card	_____
	poster	_____
	catalogue	_____
	photography	_____
	listings in newspapers & magazines	_____
	advertising	_____
	postage	_____
Preparation	framing/mounting	_____
	transport and packaging of work	_____
	insurance of work	_____
Private view	wine/beer	_____
	non-alcoholic drinks	_____
	glasses, hire/breakages	_____
	food	_____
Presentation	tools (if you are not already equipped)	_____
	screws, plugs, etc.	_____
Miscellaneous	phone calls	_____
	photocopying	_____
	stationery	_____
	travel	_____
Other	help/assistance	_____
	documentation	_____
	contingency	_____
	Total	

Possible Exhibition Income

		£
Sales	work	_____
	catalogues	_____
	drinks	_____
Funds raised	sponsorship	_____
	grants	_____
	fundraising events	
	Total	[ ]

Drawing up a budget

The above budget covers most of the expenses you may incur in organising your exhibition, and the possible income you may be able to raise. In drawing up your budget phone around for estimates, and make a note of the average cost for each item. Be prepared for unseen costs to arise, especially in the miscellaneous section, and allow a reasonable contingency of about 10% of your total costs.

Having arrived at an approximate estimate of your total income and expenditure, your next step is to decide how to cover the difference. You might decide to modify what you do to cut costs. If you are working as a group, you may decide to split costs and finance the exhibition yourselves. Or try to raise funds from other sources.

If you decide you need financial help, there are a number of ways to raise money, but take into account the time you will need for this, since it can be considerable and raising enough money may be difficult.

However you decide to finance your event, do constantly refer to your budget. Compare your original estimates with actual costs as you go along. You may need to make modifications and you don't want to find you are unable to finance an important part of your exhibition at a later stage, or worse, that you are left with a large debt at the end.

Your initial budget will be one for an ideal world, and your income is unlikely to cover your costs. Always think that you will spend more than you expect, and be pessimistic about the amount of income you can generate.

Seeking funds

Regional arts boards

see 16 • Contacts for contact addresses for all organsiations mentioned in this section.

In England contact your regional arts board. Most have support schemes in the form of grants or awards. The visual arts officer will deal with applications. Each association will have its own deadlines, and most won't finance exhibitions that are over before the application is considered. Most boards have only a single deadline in the year so check for dates well in advance and apply in good time. Awards are generally made to 'buy time' to work towards an exhibition and/or to cover the costs of materials and publicity, but not usually to pay for gallery hire charges. Most will not normally cover the full costs of a project and will expect to see other funding. The regional arts boards deal with both visual arts and crafts.

Remember you will be in competition with many others, and only a small proportion of those who apply will be supported, so put as much effort as you can into your application.

You will need to have a clear idea of what you want to do, a detailed estimate of the expenses involved and the income your exhibition or event might generate, for example, from sales of work or sales of catalogues. You will also need some form of documentation of the work involved, usually in the form of 35mm colour slides.

The Arts Council

Regional arts boards normally only consider applications for exhibitions held within their region. However, the Arts Council does operate a 'Visual Arts Exhibitions and Events' scheme which includes exhibitions and events *'which take place in England and in more than one region'*. If you are considering organising an ambitious project which would have relevance outside your area, an exhibition which might, for example, tour the country, it is worth contacting the Art Department to see if your scheme might be considered for financial assistance. There is only one application date each year. The Arts Council deals with painting, sculpture, printmaking, photography and performance art; crafts is dealt with by the Crafts Council.

Welsh Arts Council

The Welsh Arts Council's Art Department does not offer grants to artists as it believes that *'artists themselves are responsible for their basic practice as professionals'*. It does however, offer interest-free loans to artists and craftspeople for *'any purpose to do with the professional practice of art'* which includes buying materials or preparing work for an exhibition.

The Craft and Design Department, however, does offer a number of grants for craftspeople which include preparing for, or mounting, exhibitions.

The Welsh regional arts associations operate on a smaller more local scale scale than the English regional arts boards and offer only limited schemes. Contact your regional arts association for details.

Scottish Arts Council

The Scottish Arts Council, unlike the Welsh Arts Council, does offer grants to individual artists which can be used towards the costs of mounting exhibitions. The 'small assistance grants' scheme will accept applications at any time throughout the year. Craftspeople are not eligible for Scottish Arts Council awards.

Arts Council of Northern Ireland

Awards in Northern Ireland are *'offered for specific projects or for the acquisition of equipment or materials to enable an artist* (working in any field of the arts, except crafts) *to achieve specific objectives.'*

Crafts Council

The Crafts Council has developed similar relationships with the English regional arts boards as the Arts Council, except that the Crafts Council has extended this relationship to include the Welsh Arts Council. Support will only be considered for exhibitions which tour *'to at least two venues within England and Wales, but not only within one region. Tours which also include venues in Scotland, Ireland or overseas are eligible as long as they fulfil this criterion'*. Support is also given for single venue exhibitions of major national or international importance.

Crafts in Scotland

In Scotland the Scottish Development Agency (the main funding and support body for crafts) has now been replaced with an unsatisfactory mixture of the local enterprise boards and a limited company. Made in Scotland which aims to promote the Scottish crafts industry on a commercial basis. No specific funding is available to craftspeople in Scotland.

Exhibition Payment Right

The regional arts boards in England and the Welsh Arts Council, and to a less defined extend the Arts Council of Northern Ireland (but not currently the Scottish Arts Council), promote a scheme called 'Exhibition Payment Right' or 'Exhibition Fee'. The scheme is not unified across the country and there are regional variations and quirks in the way it operates. Essentially the scheme, by making contribution towards costs, encourages public galleries to pay a fee to exhibiting artists to recompense them for allowing public access to their work. The arts funding bodies do not normally make payments directly to the artists or for artist organised exhibitions.

The local council

It is worth contacting the local councils in the area you intend to show your work. The relevant department could be 'Recreation', 'Libraries and Arts', 'Leisure' or there may be an arts development unit, museums service or local arts council. Ask if they have any money available, and what kind of support they can give. Each will be different, some may help, especially if they can see how your exhibition might benefit or interest people locally. So consider this before your approach them.

Again you will need a clear idea of your plans and costs. It is advisable to do a little local research. Ask yourself what the area and the people are like, what the politics of the local constituency are, what kind of people you are approaching, how your work might relate to the locality, or what angle you might take that would be of interest to local people.

Business sponsorship

It really is only worth considering raising money through business sponsorship if your project is a large event, involving a group of artists (sponsors rarely help individuals), and which has a wide appeal, or a particular aspect which might attract potential sponsors. Raising sponsorship is very time consuming, and you are likely to find either that most businesses do not fund arts events, of, if they do, they are inundated with requests for support. However, if you are successful, this can be a way of raising quite large sums of money.

If you decide to go ahead with fund raising give yourself plenty of time. Ideally this should be twelve to eighteen months before your exhibition. One point to take into account is that most businesses work to a particular financial year. When you apply will be important, so allow time to find out from the company when it is best to apply.

Start by thinking locally. Local industry is much more likely to consider your proposal than a large national company with no local connections. Well-known, companies are likely to be approached by many people. So ask yourself whether you have any connections with local industry, or whether there are local shops or businesses you use regularly. Does your exhibition have any relation to a product made locally, or have some relation to a big local development? What kind of links might your exhibition have with the locality or with local groups?

Begin by making a list of people you might approach for sponsorship. Phone up and find out who to write to (if you can't find out, address your letter to the Public Relations officer, which will ensure your letter reaches the right person, even if the company is too small to have a public relations department). You may be asked why you wish to contact the person concerned, and you may be told there is no chance of sponsorship. You will have to decide whether it is worth pursuing this particular company.

Write a proposal outlining your plans and explaining who you are and what you do. Keep this brief; most people won't read more than one side of an A4 sheet. Keep it straightforward, don't use jargon or abbreviations, and don't assume that the reader knows anything about artists. Detail costs, how much you are trying to raise, how much you are asking them to contribute, and if possible others you are approaching. Mention if you have been offered support by someone else; this will give you credibility, and if it is a rival firm this might elicit a positive response. If you have the support of someone well known, it can be a useful aid, so mention this too.

Offer the company acknowledgement and publicity. It is important to emphasise what benefits they will receive for their sponsorship. Try to quantify how many people will see the show, and how much publicity material you will be printing and distributing which will carry their company name and logo. Say you hope they will visit your exhibition anyway. If the venue you intend using, or your exhibition, is unusual in any way (especially if you can get this across through photographs), try to persuade them to visit you or the space. This encourages a more personal interest.

If you don't receive a reply to your letter within about ten days, follow up with a phone call. Ask if they have received it, what they think, and whether you could see them to discuss the proposal. If you can deal personally with someone they are more likely to help, and if this doesn't yield results first time round, they may remember you in future.

Finally, when approaching anyone who doesn't know you, you are likely to have better results if you speak directly to the person concerned, even if this is only over the phone. A much greater understanding of you and your ideas can be gained through conversation. Don't rely upon an offer of sponsorship given over the phone or in conversation – make sure you have an agreement in writing. Keep a written record of what has been promised over the phone and if you don't get any written confirmation from the firm, write to them detailing the substance of your telephone conversation.

Trust funds
'The Directory of Grant Making Trusts' published by the Charities Aid Foundation, which lists all charitable trusts can be found in reference

libraries. It is complicated and you may need help in using it. Most trusts will only consider assisting registered charities. However, small local trusts may take an interest in you, and educational trusts may consider helping if your exhibition has an educational value. For example, you see 14 • During the exhibition might decide to organise workshops with local schools and youth clubs. Find out which local schools or clubs might be interested in the idea, and draw up a list and a proposal before you approach the trust concerned. The local council or information centre should be able to provide you with a list of local trust funds.

Advertising space

You might think about selling advertising space (if your publicity material can accommodate it), in your catalogue or on your poster.

This is probably only worth trying if you are organising a large event which is likely to attract a wide audience. Potential advertisers will want to know they are reaching people who are likely to take an interest in their product or service. If you have tried someone for sponsorship, but have been refused, it may be worth going back and asking them to advertise instead. Previous contact often helps.

You need to make sure your publicity is well designed to accommodate adverts without it conflicting with your publicity information and you will need to allow plenty of time to phone, firstly to find your advertisers (look through the 'Yellow Pages' or a local business directory), and to chase payments (some may never be paid).

Before contacting potential advertisers, decide how much space you will allocate to each advert and how much you will charge. Or you could have a range of sizes and prices. Explain to advertisers that they must supply you with 'camera-ready artwork' within a particular size limit, and well in advance of the date your publicity material goes to the printers. This means you will not need to design or typeset their advert; it should be presented to you as it will appear in your publicity, so you are not involved in any extra expense. Bear in mind that the cost to a company designing and preparing an advertisement will be more than the advertising space itself, but some may have a standard advertisement.

Help or sponsorship in kind

You may find 'help in kind' (the donation of a particular product or a large discount on materials) is more readily available. If you need to paint your space, for example, a local paint firm might be prepared to supply paint in exchange for an acknowledgement on publicity material and at the venue. You might also be able to enlist some specialist advice or help, free of charge, which could save you money. If you need a particular product or material for your work, the manufacturers may be persuaded to provide it.

People are often more prepared to give something they already have, rather than money.

Fund-raising events

You might decide to organise some kind of event to raise money, for example, a disco, jumble sale or cabaret. This can be a good way of raising small sums. But these events can lose you money if they are not well organised. Try to assess the costs involved before you begin, and keep an eye on the fund-raising throughout the event. Think too of the time involved.

Conclusion

In conclusion, raising funds can be a difficult and time consuming task, especially if you have no previous experience. However, artists have been known to raise quite large sums and, of course, having sufficient funds available will give you much more choice about how you organise your exhibition. Success will depend very much on the type of project, how it relates to those you are approaching for funds, and how well you present your application. You will usually be up against a lot of competition, so it is important to allow a considerable amount of time and thought.

6 • Timetable

About four months before your exhibition is due to open, draw up a timetable. To do this, work backwards from your private view date. For example, allow one or two days for hanging, invitation cards to arrive at their destination ten days before, four days for second class posting, four weeks for printing, and so on.

Approach organisations for funding and companies for sponsorship a year in advance of your exhibition, if possible. Approach schools, colleges, authorities, etc to set up any educational activities at least six months in advance of your show.

Example timetable

1 February	Phone publications for copy deadlines
2-15 February	Prepare and send press packs
16-18 February	Prepare and send listings information to magazines
15 March	Prepare artwork for invitation cards
1 April	Artwork for invitation cards to printers
3 April	Start framing
14 April	Send out press/media invitations
19 April	Press/media invitations to arrive
30 April	Organise transport to gallery
1 May	Post rest of invitations
2 May	Arrange insurance for exhibition
5 May	Invitations to arrive
6 May	Organise arrangements for private view
7 May	Put up posters/cards locally
14/15 May	Hanging
15 May	Private view
16 May-5 June	Exhibition dates
20 May	Organise transport of work from gallery
6 June	Take down exhibition

7 • Publicity

If you choose to exhibit your work, you want to make the most of the situation. Use this opportunity to attract attention to your work, to extend your audience and your contacts, and to open up opportunities for the future. The only way to attract visitors is through publicity; if people don't know about your show, they won't come.

Publicity need not necessarily be expensive. Depending on the nature of your work and your resources, you might choose a very professional or highly polished look or, alternatively, a more casual or unconventional approach. But whatever the style you adopt, make sure your publicity suits your work and is well produced.

If your exhibition is not well publicised, you will probably be disappointed. Good publicity, on the other hand, can make your exhibition a success, and continue to work for you in the future. Think of the whole experience as one of many which will help build your reputation in the eyes of your audience.

So put everything you can into publicity and make all your other efforts worthwhile.

Promotion

Listings

An inexpensive way to advertise your exhibition is through listings in magazines. These provide brief details about your exhibition, and many publications offer free listings or make a small charge. Make the most of these, they reach a wide audience and may attract visitors at no extra cost.

Consider who you want to reach and so which publications you use. Art magazines reach artists, those involved in the arts, and those with a continuous interest in the arts. *City Limits* and *Time Out* (in London) reach a wider range of people including tourists, visitors to the city, regular readers with an interest in the arts in general, and those interested in alternatives to established venues. Local listings run by councils and local papers reach people nearest to your venue, but only a small proportion of readers will be interested in your type of event. see 17 • Further reading Artists' newsletters will reach mainly other artists. *Artist Newsletter* published by AN Publications is the most widely distributed, but there are others. Some are run locally by artists and some regional arts boards publish newsletters too.

About three months before your exhibition, phone around and make a list of copy deadlines. Allow plenty of time, as some are well in advance of publication dates, and some publications come out infrequently.

Type your details carefully: your name(s), name, address and telephone number of the space, opening times and dates, and perhaps a title or a few words to give some idea of what it is.

A week after sending information, phone and speak to whoever compiles the listings. Ask if they have received your letter and if they will be able to include your details. This is especially important with publications such as *Time Out* and *City Limits,* since they have limited space and don't guarantee to include everything. If there is a choice to be made and they remember speaking to you it might tip the balance in your favour.

Even if a certain publication doesn't include anything first time around, next time you exhibit try again and remind them who you are. Familiarity with your name may pay off eventually.

Advertisements

Advertisements can be placed in all kinds of publications and they attract more attention than a simple listings entry alongside many others, but this can be costly.

Begin by deciding who you are trying to reach and choose the most appropriate publications. Phone for prices (these will be quite varied) and for deadlines for receipt of artwork. How much you are prepared to spend will probably help you decide which to choose.

see 'Invitation cards', below You can either design your advert and provide artwork of to the required size or get the publishers to set it for you, though this will cost you extra.

Remember that the costs involved include the 'origination' of the artwork before you pay for the advertising space itself.

Editorial coverage

You may decide you want to seek more extensive press coverage. If you are successful, it can greatly increase the number of people who attend your exhibition, and an article published about your work could lead to more sales. You won't have to pay for such coverage, but it is difficult and time consuming to achieve, and you need to spend some money in attracting interest.

This kind of press coverage can take two forms. You could persuade someone to publish something about your exhibition before it begins as a news item or feature, or you might find someone prepared to come along to the show and review it.

There are dozens of publications to choose from. Approach art magazines, national papers with arts pages, the Sunday supplements, other specialist magazines which have arts pages, the local press and free handout sheets. AN Publications 'Fact Pack 3: Mailing the Press' gives contact addresses for art magazines and national and regional press. You will find it extremely difficult to get national press coverage unless you or the venue are well known, or you know someone who writes for, say, a national newspaper. It is less difficult to attract the local press, so you might decide to concentrate on local publications, especially early on in your career.

see17 • Further reading

Each publication works to different deadlines, so start months in advance. Phone each publication you are interested in and find out how far in advance their copy date is, and the name of the person who will be dealing with your material.

Press packs

You need to put together a package which can be sent to the publications you are interested in. This needs to look interesting and professional as you are competing with many galleries with specialist marketing managers and marketing budgets.

Think about what type of publication(s) you are approaching and what would be likely to persuade them to publish something, judging by past issues. For instance the local press might be especially interested if there is some particular relevance to the locality. Art publications will of course be more interested in the artistic content of the exhibition.

Your package should include a letter and/or press release, photographs and your curriculum vitae. You could substitute colour photocopies or colour postcards if you are sending to a number of places and you should include a note saying that black & white photographs and/or colour transparencies are available on request, but only say this if they are available – magazines and press are likely to want them at very short notice – there may not have time to get some processed.

Press release

A press release is a statement about you and your work, linked to a particular event, which is sent out to the press and media. A press release is designed to attract the attention of those who receive it and, if successful, it may be used word for word.

If a sympathetic supporter will write a press release for you, this can be helpful, especially if it is someone whose reputation is respected by the person receiving your material. If you can't find someone else to write it, have a go yourself.

Put some time into writing it, but keep it fairly short – 250 words is a maximum. Any more than an A4 sheet is unlikely to be read. Make sure you include all the relevant details about your exhibition in the first paragraph. Subsequent paragraphs should be about the event/work. Point out anything unusual or of particular interest about you, the work, the venue or the event – make it brief but punchy. Take into account the type of audience you are trying to reach, for example, would the readers have any knowledge of contemporary art? Type your press release, and use double spacing, which leaves room for notes or underlining by anyone who uses it. Include a date, a contact name and telephone number.

Whenever you send out anything you want returned, label each item with your name and address; photographs can easily be separated from letters. Enclose a stamped addressed envelope. Mark the outside of this envelope with the name of the publication you are sending it to, as some publications return material with no mention of who they are, and you will want to keep track of who has or hasn't returned material. If your material has not been returned by the start of your exhibition, you need to chase up with phone calls. Some publications take time to return unsolicited material, but the longer you leave chasing it up, the more likelihood there is of it going astray. If you don't get photographs returned, it is expensive to replace them.

You may find, especially the first time around, that little or nothing is published. But it is worth persevering. Familiarity with your name may eventually bring results.

Photographs

Include some photographs of the work in your package. Send photographs rather than slides – they are easier to look at. If the magazine reproduces in monotone send black and white photographs, preferably glossy and about 8"x10". If the venue is of particular interest, send a photograph of this as well. If you are approaching the local press, include a photograph of yourself with your work, it is more likely to be used. Consider how your work comes across as a black and white reproduction. If it is abstract, and colour is an important element, it may be better to include a photograph of several pieces of work in their surroundings, to help give the work a context.

Curriculum Vitae

A curriculum vitae is a brief account of your career to date. It is used to inform people about you, for example, when you make an application for something which relates to your career as an artist.

Always type your CV, unless you have exceptionally good handwriting. Set it out clearly and divide it into sections so anyone reading it can easily see the sequence of events in your career, and can see where to find the information they want.

Begin with your name, address and telephone number, your studio address and phone number (if you have one, and if you don't it would be useful to include a number at which you can be reached), your date and place of birth, and details of your art education. In the next section, list details of your exhibitions in chronological order. Put the date (year) at the left hand side of the page, then the title of the exhibition, if any, or state that it was a one-person or two-person show, name the gallery and the city. You can list one person exhibitions separately from group shows. Another section would be your bibliography, which lists details of any items published about your work. Include the name of the publication, the issue date or number, title of article and author.

Other sections should detail any experience or information which relates to your career: awards received, collections which include your work, art teaching and other related working experience such as any residencies and commissions.

Of course, early in your career your curriculum vitae will be short, but don't let this deter you from setting it out well. Anyone looking at your CV will be more impressed if you take time and trouble in informing them of what you have done.

If you are lucky enough to have something written about your exhibition, use this to build for the future. Collect any cuttings you have. Copies of these may be useful for other purposes. Include each item published in the bibliography on your curriculum vitae. When you show again, follow up those publications which wrote something about you previously.

Printed material

There are two main reasons for producing printed publicity material. Firstly, to attract attention, and secondly, to provide the necessary information so your audience can attend. Your choice of publicity material is determined by who you are trying to attract and the costs involved. Before making any decisions have a good look at other people's publicity – cards you have received, posters on notice boards, etc. This will help to get your imagination going but use the opportunity to be critical.

The usual way to produce publicity material involves deciding what form of material you want (posters, invitation/announcement cards, leaflets, broadsheets, etc), what information you want included, some idea of how you want it to look, and how much you can afford to spend. You then employ a designer to come up with several designs from which you can choose. The designer then produces the artwork which they or you present to the printer. The printer then prints the material.

However, employing professionals at every stage like this is expensive, and the extent to which you need to varies. This section suggests many combinations of the use of your own skills and those of professionals.

Invitation cards

An important way of informing people about your exhibition is to have an invitation card printed. Receiving a personal invitation like this is the most likely way to attract a potential visitor. This need not necessarily be expensive, but you want to achieve as good a result as possible within your budget. Your card can be very simple – black text on white card, or it can be a colour reproduction of your work, which is much more expensive. There are many other options between these two. Whatever kind of card you decide on, it needs to be appropriate to your work and well produced.

The costs involved depend on how much of the work you can do for yourself, and at what point you need to bring in a professional. At every stage consider whether you can do it yourself, or have a friend who can help.

Firstly you need to decide on the kind of card you want. It could be text on its own, or text and an image. It could be one colour (ie black and white) or full colour. It could be printed both sides ('backed-up') or on one side only.

What you decide depends partly on how much you can afford. But if this is to be your main form of publicity, spend as much as you can on it.

Consider who will be receiving your cards and what effect you want them to have. If you are trying to attract those who don't know you or your work, it is important to have an illustration. Depending on the nature of your work this may need to be in colour or it may reproduce well in black and white. A high degree of tonal contrast would probably result in a good black and white reproduction.

Consider what you want on the back of the card? You'll probably want your name and the title, size and detail of the work illustrated (and some method for indicating which way up the work is), as well as any credit necessary for the photographer. Do you want your address and telephone number, or any further information about yourself? What do you want to use the card for; does it have a useful life after the exhibition? Will it be a postcard with space for handwritten message and address, a straight invitation card, or can you also use it as your business card. If the back is laid out in the right way it can be used to serve several functions. Remember that you can overprint a postcard at a later date, so that out of a print run of 1000 you could use 200 as invitation cards by overprinting them.

If you are inviting people who are unlikely to know the area where you are showing, consider including a map indicating the venue in relation to public transport and any local landmarks, particularly if it is not easy to find. If you intend using your card for notice boards, remember your card will be surrounded by many other, often larger, posters and notices. So try to come up with an image or design which draws attention to your card.

You need to decide how many cards to have printed. Try to assess how many people you want to invite and then double it. You are bound to have forgotten people, and you may find other opportunities to give out cards. It costs only a little more to have, say, 500 printed than 200. So it is worth having as many printed as you can, within reason.

Before making final decisions, phone a couple of printers (in the 'Yellow Pages' or local directories) and compare prices for different kinds of cards (text only, text and black and white image, colour, etc) and sizes. Tell them roughly how many you need and ask how many more you could have printed for the same price, or a little extra. Normally, printers will quote for, say, 500 and then give the price for extra runs of 500. The extra print-run is known as a 'run-on'.

see 'Postcard printers', 16 • Contacts

Artwork

Artwork is the final visual material which is reproduced by the printer. If this is badly prepared, then the printing and final result will also be bad. When the artwork is camera-ready, ie the way you want it to look in the end, it is photographed by the printer, plates made up and the card printed off from the plates.

Artwork: do-it-yourself

You may decide to prepare all the artwork yourself. In theory this is the cheapest way. But in practice, especially if you have no experience, it can be an expensive mistake. If you decide to do it all yourself, be prepared to spend considerable time on it – artwork must be well prepared for a professional result.

Start by considering the overall design; how you can arrange the information clearly. If you are having an image, where will it be? Is the design interesting? Make a rough drawing, making sure you include everything, and refer to this as you are working on the real thing.

If you have not designed a card before, have a look at those produced by other artists or galleries. Consider what attracts you about them and try to use this in your own design.

Text

You can often do this quite easily yourself. If you have good handwriting this can be an attractive and simple way of making your text. If you have access to an electric typewriter with several typefaces, word processor or desk-top-publishing equipment, you may decide to type your text. There are also many types of 'instant lettering' like Letraset available, but if you are going to use Letraset, allow plenty of time. You will need to do lots of measuring, and be patient in getting the spacing of both the letters and the words correct. Make sure the letters are exactly in line. Do some practice tests first and photocopy them to give you an idea of what the results might be. Any hint of uneven spacing or misaligned letters will show up even more in the end result.

Keep text brief, don't include unnecessary wording, but include:

* name(s) of artist(s),
* type of work/title of exhibition,
* exhibition dates,
* opening times and days,
* private view date and times,
* any acknowledgement to funding bodies or sponsors, and
* image caption, ie title, date, medium and size of work illustrated, which way up it is and any credits for the photographer.

Your card may look more interesting, and can be more easily read if you use more than one size or weight (ie light, medium or bold) of lettering. You may want to emphasise your name with bolder type, or differentiate between the dates of the exhibition and the dates of the private view with italics, and so on.

Check all your spelling and details are correct, then get someone else to check.

Image

What kind of image do you want and how will you make it? It could be a photograph of your work, or the venue, or something that relates to your work. It could be a drawing, an etching or a print you've already made, or something you make especially for your card. It could be a photograph of yourself. Whatever you choose, keep in mind that its function is to attract attention and inform.

If you are going to use a photograph, the cheapest way is to take it yourself. But remember when your image is printed it can lose at least 10% of its definition, so you want to begin with as good a photograph as possible. If you have good photographs, use them.

If your image is to be in black and white, for best results have a 10"x8" print made and have the printer reduce this to the final size. Although it can be slightly cheaper to present the printer with a photograph the actual size you want it reproduced. If you need to have a photograph enlarged or reduced to fit a space on the card, but you do not have access to a darkroom, enquire at a good photography shop or film processors. This shouldn't be expensive, especially if you require a standard size.

Whoever is making the print for you, tell them it is for reproduction, this will need to be taken into account by the processor.

If you are having a full-colour image you need a colour slide or transparency, the larger the better. The cheapest way is to take this yourself, but you need a good slide with accurate colour and pin-point focus, so if you are not experienced in photography it may pay to have someone take it for you. As the cost of colour printing is high, you must make sure the photograph or transparency is of good quality, otherwise you will be wasting your money.

Presenting the printer with a colour slide of your work is the best way to achieve accurate colour gradation during the printing process. But some printers may prefer you to provide a colour photograph. If you do it this way, provide the printer with a colour slide as well, and explain that the slide is an accurate reproduction of the colour in your work. This helps the printer to achieve a better result.

A proof

A proof is a sample print, which is run off and allows you to see the result before all the cards are printed. It adds a to the overall cost. It should not be necessary if your card is to be printed in one colour, but if you are having a 'full' colour image it is important as it is difficult for the printer to achieve a good colour balance first time off. Seeing a proof is the only way to ensure you end up with a satisfactory result. At the proofing stage, adjustments to the colour can be made before it is finally printed. Chromalin proofs are an alternative and cheaper method of obtaining proofs but as these are not sample prints can not be used to accurately check colour balance; they are more useful to check whether text wanted in a particular colour has been processed correctly.

Artwork: prepared professionally

If you already know a graphic artist, or have a friend who has done this type of thing before, this may be a good way to have your artwork done. But before committing yourself, ask to see examples of previous work. It can be difficult to tell a friend the result is not up to scratch, especially if they are giving you a discount.

At the same time, ask for an estimate of the cost, and discuss the possibility that the job will take longer than expected. How might this affect the cost? If you decide this is the best option, you will probably still be responsible for the design of the card. You need to present the person concerned with a drawing which shows clearly what you have in mind, and make sure all details and spelling are correct.

You might choose to employ a professional photographer to make the slide or photograph of your work. This is more expensive than taking it yourself, but the result should be very good. Don't be afraid of asking them to do it again, at no extra charge, if you are not happy with the result.

You can have your artwork prepared entirely by the printer, and some may be able to photograph your work for you. This is more expensive, but in the long run you may decide it is worth the extra cost to save time and trouble. Also, if the printer provides you with a quotation, whatever the problems, the artwork should be supplied at the price quoted. Remember if you have text on both sides of the card, this may double the price of the artwork preparation.

If the printer does prepare your artwork, it will look professional, but you may find you have less control over the end result. The printer may have different ideas from you about what looks good.

You need to provide the printer with a drawing which details the basic design and position of the text and image. All details must be correct, including spelling; the printer may not even correct obvious mistakes. Indicate what kind of lettering you want for each line. Do you want capital letters throughout, just at the beginning of words or not at all? Do you want bolder type here or there and what kind of type faces would you like?

It is important to ask to see the artwork before the plate is made and printing begins. When you see the finished artwork, take your time and check for mistakes. Has all the information been included? Do you like the overall result? If you are not happy in any way, ask for adjustments to be made. This is easily done.

If you have considerable funds at your disposal, you can use a designer to organise the whole thing for you. The designer acts on your instructions and is responsible for the design, the preparation of the artwork, organising the printing and instructing the printer. If you use a designer you should expect a high quality look to your card and this is the most expensive way to have a card produced.

Printing

If you are organising the printing of your card, your first step is to phone around for estimates (do this before you decide how to have your artwork done, the printer may give you a good price for artwork or typesetting if you are just having text). You can find printers in the Yellow Pages, local resource directories, through friends or through local galleries and art centres. A personal recommendation from someone you trust is always best, so try asking around.

Probably the best way to get an accurate quotation is to visit a printer, if there is one nearby. You can take along your design, or another card which is similar to what you want, and discuss it face to face.

Before you approach a printer, have a clear idea of what you require. If you need full colour, ask for the cost of a proof be included in the quotation as a separate item. Ask about all the possible extra costs there might be for artwork, photography, enlarging or reducing, for having both sides printed, more than one colour, and anything out of the ordinary you want. Ask how many you can have printed for the price and get a breakdown of the estimate so you know how much each part is costing you. This helps you decide how much you should ask the printer to do. Ask for an estimate for more than one size if your design is flexible. This can make quite a difference to the cost, as standard size card is cheaper. The usual sizes are A6 which is post-card size, and A5 which is twice that size.

Some specialist printers offer cheaper colour cards as they will probably be making one plate with many images for several different clients. This considerably reduces the cost and can produce perfectly good results, but will not guarantee accuracy in the reproduction of the colours. Some do send out proofs but the printer will be averaging out the colour balance across the several images and can not attend too closely to a single image.

A thousand A6 postcards printed full-colour one side and black text on reverse, from such a specialist postcard printer will cost between £140 and £190. This price might include proofs but watch out for any extras such as laminating or varnishing which may be quoted separately.

When you have decided what your card will be like, enquire how long the job will take. A realistic time to allow would be two to three weeks. If the printer quotes less time (especially with colour work), be prepared for it to take longer than quoted. Some will do a rush job if you really need it, but you may have to pay more, and if you do without a proof to save time you may not get the quality you hoped for. Arrange to go in and discuss your requirements in detail.

When you go along, take some invitation cards with you, either your own from previous shows, or from another artist or gallery. This helps to give the printer an idea of the quality you require. Some printers are not used to doing work for artists, and where an illustration is required, artists need a greater degree of accuracy than many other clients. Make it clear you need a good reproduction of your work and ask how well your image will reproduce, especially if you are using an original drawing or print.

Check the printer understands all your requirements and ask for a written quotation. The price quoted at this stage is the price you will pay at the end, unless you make major changes to the original agreement. But ask whether the price includes VAT and whether or not the item is zero rated. The VAT rules for printing are complex and it is impossible to give a short explanation of them, always check with the printer to ensure that the bill does not end up 17.5% more than you had expected.

The quality of the card used is also important. Discuss with the printer the type and weight of card, and surface finish (lamination, varnish glazing) you need. Compare a sample with examples you have. The thinnest you should accept is 250gsm, and if you intend sending your card as a post-card, ie without an envelope, the weight needs to be at least 300gsm (gsm means grammes per square metre).

Ask when your proof will be ready and make a note of all the details you need to remember. Take a sample of card to be used away with you.

Phone to see if your proof is ready before you go in to see it. When you go, take the sample of card, the details you wrote down and an old invitation card with you, in case you need to compare quality of image.

Take a good look at your proof. Take your time and check all the information is included, that the spelling and details are correct, the layout and design are as you specified, any illustration is satisfactory, the colour accurate, the image sharp etc, and that the correct card has been used.

If any changes need to be made, or you are not happy in any way, say so. Some printers may suggest it is too difficult or not worth the trouble to make alterations. But be firm, as long as you were clear from the outset, you should end up with what you want - you are paying and you want to be happy with the result so you feel good about people receiving it.

Before you leave, ask when the finished cards will be ready. Telephone to check before you go in to collect them. When you go in note that changes you asked for have been made, and the cards have been trimmed to the correct size. Make sure the cards were dry before being guillotined and that the ink hasn't transferred ('set-off') from one card to the next. If there are any mistakes or the cards are badly cut or guillotined, as long as your original artwork was clear, you are entitled to have them redone at no extra cost. If it is too close to the start of your exhibition for this to be done, ask for a reduction in the price. This is not ideal, but better than nothing. Pay when you are happy to take the cards away with you.

Poster

Having a card to publicise your exhibition is really a basic necessity, but you may also like to have a poster. It is nice if you can afford it, but is it worth the extra expense? A lot depends upon who you are trying to reach, and where you intend to publicise.

Most of your visitors will be attracted by personal invitations, or through listings, and you may choose simply to have your cards pinned up on notice boards. Of course a poster will demand more attention on a crowded notice board and some people will undoubtedly be attracted to your show by seeing a poster, especially locally. So if you are going to publicise widely in the locality or intend sending information to many large art venues, you may feel a poster is worth the extra expense.

If you decide to have a poster as well as a card, you can use the same basic design and wording, so you can save by having them printed at the same time and by using the same artwork. It is easier for the printer to scale down, rather than up, and the result will be better. Scaling up can show up any imperfections.

The problem with using the same artwork for your poster as your card, is that an invitation card and poster are designed to do different things. A good looking card may make a very uninteresting poster.

If you are designing a poster from scratch, remember it will often be seen surrounded by many others so a striking design is more likely to stand out.

Think about the size of your poster – the larger it is, the more expensive it is likely to be. But good design can compensate for a smaller size.

Normally cards and posters are printed by a commercial process known as offset litho. This is the most common printing process and is ideal for very long runs (ie large numbers). However, silkscreen printing is another way of making a poster. A silkscreen poster can be an artwork in itself. The process can produce a wide variety of effects and intense colours. But as each one is usually hand printed this is a time consuming and expensive way to produce a poster. It is certainly worth considering if you only need a small number, or are involved in a big event and can afford them. If they are attractive and printed on good quality paper you might also be able to sell them.

The choice, of course, must depend on what is most appropriate for your work. If you want a good reproduction of, for example, a painting, then offset litho is likely to be your first choice. A small run of posters, using bold typography, strong colour and an abstract design will be ideally suited to silkscreening.

Look around at other posters and see what other artists or galleries have chosen. Think carefully about the impression you want to make.

Catalogue

A catalogue at its simplest is a list of works on show; simply typed and copied. At the other end of the scale, it can be a glossy printed publication with colour reproductions and essays on the work.

Again, what you do depends on your finances. Having a hundred copies of a typed sheet may cost only a few pounds, and provides basic information about the works. But you may decide to have something a little more expensive, especially if your exhibition is to be a big event involving many people. It is certainly a nice extra to have, since, besides attracting attention at the time of the exhibition, it will provide a permanent record and may help promote your work in the future.

If you decide to have something a little more sophisticated than a typed sheet, you can make the most of your catalogue by using it to attract the attention of those who would probably not otherwise make the effort to see your show. For example, national critics, who might just be persuaded if they receive something out of the ordinary. It is also something which might be sent to arts organisations like the arts councils, regional arts boards, commercial galleries, collectors and others who might be able to buy work or help with finance.

Your catalogue can be all kinds of shapes and sizes, so again, take a look at others before you settle on what you would like. You could just have a printed cover and slip in typed and duplicated sheets of information, or you can go the whole way and have bound catalogues.

If you are able to afford a good catalogue it is important to employ a professional designer, as it can be complex to put together. But generally, follow the same procedures as with any other printed publicity material.

If it is to be printed, you need to start planning well in advance. If you are going to make the most of it, it needs to be ready, ideally, a month before your exhibition begins, so there is time to send it to those who might be interested and attracted by a catalogue.

Cutting costs

If you are exhibiting alone, at short notice, or on a very low budget, an inexpensive alternative is to use a photocopier to produce all your publicity material. It is only worth considering this if you do not intend to send out a large number of cards or posters, as the costs per copy will rise proportionately, unlike printing which becomes cheaper the more you do.

If you decide to do something this way, try to find a local resource centre where you can make copies at a cheaper rate than in, for example, a stationers. Your local library may be able to help. A local school, college or community project may let you use theirs, so ask around. You might also try negotiating a reduced price for quantity at a stationers or high street copy shop.

You will need to spend some time experimenting on the photocopier, so build this into the estimate of costs. Try experimenting with collage, drawing on the spot, changes in light and darkness, with enlargement or reduction the use of images, photographs, drawings. Have a look at all the things the copier can do; some even do colour. If you are doing just a few posters, you might even colour them individually for greater effect.

I have seen some very attractive results produced on a photocopier. But put a good deal of thought into your design, because it can look shoddy if you are not careful. You can afford a little time and expense in working out the design, as once this is worked out, it is quick and cheap to make the copies. The whole thing can be done in a day and, depending on where, for a few pounds.

There are other cheap and effective ways of making publicity material. You could try looking for a local resource where you could make your own screen printed posters and invitation cards. A community centre print workshop might let you use their facilities for example. Your local council should be able to tell you what exists in their area. You could try a local college art department, if there is one. The local education authority might also be able to help – many run art courses with facilities available. You might even set something up at home yourself. You need very little equipment to make posters from lino cuts or monoprints (although making monoprints will be time consuming if you need a large number).

With any method which is new to you, allow enough time and materials to experiment until you feel confident with it.

There are all sorts of ways of making publicity material. It is up to you to look at the possibilities available to you and to decide how you can best publicise your exhibition.

Remember your publicity material is the key way to attract visitors to your exhibition, so put all you've got into ensuring good results. It can be cheaply and simply produced, but it must always fulfil its functions of attracting and informing your potential audience, it must be well produced and suited to your work and approach. Be alert to all the little things that can go wrong, and constantly check details. Keep an eye on what the printer does, especially one who is not used to doing work for artists and be on your guard for those who might cut corners. Good publicity can go on working for you long after the exhibition is over, and give you the pleasure and satisfaction of having something done well.

Mailing

Your first question is: 'Who do I want to inform about the show?' Your mailing will probably fall into three basic categories: the media, who could give you further publicity; galleries, arts organisations and art colleges, who could offer you other opportunities; friends and artists who you already know and who are supportive of your work.

The media - critics/press/radio/television
This category includes everybody from the national art critics who write regularly in the daily and weekend newspapers and weekly journals, the specialised art magazine critics, those who write about art in more general publications to journalists on local papers, national and local radio and television arts presenters.

Many in this category, especially the national newspaper, TV and radio critics, will be difficult to attract through mailing, unless you have some personal contact, or you or the venue already have an established reputation. Those who work in the media are constantly bombarded by invitations to exhibitions and they can only give coverage to a tiny fraction of them. However, while you might not expect a national critic to respond early in your career, you might get coverage from a local publication or a local radio station.

It is worth persevering and mailing the media each time you exhibit your work. Familiarity with your name may eventually bring results. But don't be too disappointed if you get no response at first.

You can compile a media mailing list by looking through publications for the names of those who review or write about arts events. TV and Radio Times will list those who introduce arts programmes. Address the envelope to the person concerned, and to the section of the publication to which they contribute, or the programme they are involved with. If you can get hold of home addresses, this is obviously preferable, but difficult unless you have personal contact. So otherwise mail to the publication, television or radio station address. AN Publications publishes information sheets listing contact addresses for art magazines, national and regional newspapers, TV and radio companies.

see 17 • Further reading

Aim to mail the media about three weeks before your private view. If anyone does decide to write something, this will at least give them a little time. If you haven't already sent information about yourself, include a letter or press release.

see 'Press packs', above

Galleries/arts organisations/art colleges

This category includes the major public and commercial galleries, local and alternative exhibition spaces, public funding bodies and other arts organisations and colleges. The people in this category may be in a position to offer you opportunities in the future.

It is important not just to concentrate on those who work for national organisations and major galleries, as they are unlikely to come if you and your work are unknown to them. It is still worth sending out cards and posters (if you have them) to these places, since, if your publicity is displayed, all their visitors have a chance to see it. You might expect someone from some of the local exhibition spaces to come, and find out who is the visual arts officer of your local regional arts association, who is the local council's arts and recreation officer, and who is on the advisory panels to these organisations.

Mail venues outside of the town or city you are showing in, especially if it is London, since many directors and organisers make regular trips to London, and you never know when they might fit in a trip to see your work if they find your publicity attractive or interesting.

Think about who you are going to mail and why. For example, it is not worth mailing a commercial gallery which promotes work of a very different kind to your own, but it is worth mailing galleries that put on exhibitions you like or of work which is sympathetic to your own.

If you would like your publicity displayed on a notice board include a note requesting this. If you are using your card as a poster, don't forget to send two if both sides have been printed. Send a third card to the director, organiser or head of department. Try to find out their names and address the envelopes accordingly.

A list of galleries in London, and some of the larger regional galleries, can be compiled from the bi-monthly New Exhibitions of Contemporary Art which can be picked up in most London galleries. You can also look through art magazine listings. A more comprehensive guide to galleries, country wide, can be compiled from the 'Directory of see 17 • Further reading Exhibition Spaces' published by AN Publications. Major arts organisations are listed in 'Arts Address Book' published by Peter Marcan, and regional arts boards or local council arts and recreation departments can provide you with a list of local venues.

If you are interested in teaching, make an effort with all the colleges and art departments within travelling distance of your show. Find out who the heads of department are, and with your card include a letter about your work and some slides. A list of Fine Art courses can be obtained from the Council for National Academic Awards which can be found in the London telephone directory.

Wherever possible address your envelope to a particular person rather than to the organisation in general.

Even if you do not attract any of these people to your exhibition this time round, they may remember your name on future occasions. If your card or poster is particularly attractive it may be left pinned up permanently, giving you continuous free publicity.

Friends/artists

This is of course the group most likely to respond and support you and it is worth making sure as many as possible come to see your work. It is also important to mail to other artists you don't know, especially if you admire their work. Many artists sit on selection panels, advise arts organisations or organise events themselves.

Finally always include in your mailing anyone who has expressed an interest in your work or bought work from you in the past.

Your mailing list

A good mailing list is a valuable asset. Don't draw up a new one each time you exhibit. Keep a permanent mailing list which you add to and up-date continuously. If you keep your mailing list in order, it is much easier than starting from scratch each time and you are much less likely to forget someone. Get into the habit of automatically noting possible new additions to your list, or revising it if you discover someone has moved. Be careful, though, not to let your mailing list become too big. It should be fairly comprehensive but not wasteful. Remember a mailing of 500 will cost you £85 at 17p second class post. It can be useful to compare mailing lists with other artists and swop useful names and addresses, but don't just copy someone else's list – it may not be relevant to you. You should be aware of who each person on your list is, what they do and why you have included them.

If you compile a mailing list you intend using over and over, it is worth getting properly organised from the start. There are various ways of doing this. One simple method is to purchase A4 sheets of sticky labels from a good quality stationer. There will be a ruled sheet of paper with the labels, divided into rectangles the size of the labels. Place the ruled sheet under a sheet of typing paper, type a name and address in each rectangle. You then have A4 sheets of names and addresses which can be photocopied onto the sheets of labels each time you need to do a mailing. This does involve some expense, but in the long run it saves a good deal of time.

Keep your mailing list divided into sections so you can easily add to it and make changes. This also allows you to use only one section at certain times without wasting a lot of labels. You could divide it into the following sections:

- Media - national
- Media - local
- Galleries - London
- Galleries - regional
- Galleries - local
- Arts organisations - national
- Arts organisations - regional
- Arts organisations - local
- Fine art departments
- Artists
- Friends
- Art buyers
- Miscellaneous

Preparing your mailing

While you will need to mail the media about three weeks in advance of your private view, you should plan to have the rest of your cards arrive at their destination about a week or ten days before the exhibition opens. This allows some notice, but not so much that people forget.

If you are sending out several hundred cards, allow the time to prepare your mailing. Take into account that you will need to put the cards into the envelopes (unless you are using them as post-cards), you may want to include other information, you will need to address each one or stick on the address labels, and seal the envelopes. All this takes considerable time.

Think of presentation at this stage too. It may make a difference, especially to those who receive many cards. If your card is obviously one of an anonymous mailing, ie a cheap brown envelope with haphazardly placed label, your card may go unopened into the bin.

Cutting the cost of your mailing

First of all, have your mailing ready to send by second class post; allow four days for it to arrive. If you can design your card so it can be used as a post-card, this will save on the cost of envelopes and save time stuffing them too.

If you know of another artist, or artists who are showing at about the same time as you, you could consider combining your mailing. But make sure you like their material and it won't detract from yours in any way.

Local arts venues might be prepared to include at least part of your mailing with theirs. Phone around, someone may help, especially if your exhibition is nearby, or you have had some previous contact with them. Suggest at the same time that you display a poster for them. Some local arts and recreation departments might help if they have an event planned at about the same time. Do find out though, who they will be mailing and who they might send your card to.

Get into the habit of carrying some cards with you, you may be able to deliver some personally, and you may meet new people between mailing your cards and the end of your exhibition. Friends might also deliver some for you.

Local publicity

Local publicity is very important and needs to be given time and attention. Most of your visitors, apart from friends and personal contacts, are going to have some local connections. Apart from casual visitors, ie those passing by your exhibition space, any others are likely to live or work locally, or have some reason for coming to the area. It is well worth spending extra time distributing cards or posters near to your exhibition space.

Make sure all surrounding arts venues, including theatres etc. receive your publicity. In this way you may reach people with a general interest in the arts. If you have time, go round yourself and make sure cards/posters are pinned to notice boards. Make sure local libraries and tourist attractions display your publicity. You could also place cards/posters in local shops, pubs, launderettes, etc, but do ask first.

If you are going to make your local publicity work well, it is useful to include a map of the area, either on your publicity material or placed near to it. This is especially important if your exhibition space is not easy to find, or not visible from the street.

8 • Framing

Framing your work for an exhibition is very important. Don't leave it to the last minute, it requires careful consideration, and whichever way you decide to frame your work it is likely to take considerable time.

Framing your work?

There are two reasons for framing it; firstly to protect, especially if it is delicate or easy to damage and secondly, to improve presentation. Both these factors need to be taken into account when deciding whether or not to frame work, and how to do it. Watercolour, pastel or charcoal, in fact any work on paper, or which will not stand up to a curious or careless audience, will need protection.

Protection of work is a practical concern; presentation is a matter of taste. The way you frame your work will depend on the nature of the work and how you want it to be seen. Your work may be highly finished or very loose and this will effect the way you frame it. If you are framing a number of works, you may want the frames to be uniform, or you may want each to be individual.

There is no 'right' way to frame work. The questions are: Does your framing adequately protect your work? Does it enhance its presentation? Are you properly in control of the results? Can you afford it? Spend some time thinking about this and look at how other artists and galleries frame work and compare the costs of the various methods.

Works on paper

Mounts

You will need to decide how you are going to mount your work. There are several ways of doing this. You can simply take a piece of backing board and mount your work onto this. The backing board can either be slightly larger than the work so that when framed, the work 'floats' inside the frame or it can be the same size as the work, so the edges of the work will be overlapped by the frame by about an eighth of an inch to half an inch, depending on the frames rebate.

Alternatively, you can use a window mount. You can mount the work on a backing board first, and then add a window mount which is a little bigger than the work so the work is 'floating' inside. Otherwise, the mount can be cut a little smaller than the work and overlap the edges of the work by between one eighth of an inch and a quarter of an inch. The work will be taped to the back of the mount.

There are, of course, many variations to these basic mounts. You might wish to crop a work through the use of a window mount or your work might be an unusual shape and need to be dealt with in a very particular way.

Making window mounts

You can make window mounts yourself. This isn't difficult to do, but if you haven't made mounts before, practise with spare pieces of card before you begin on the real thing. You need good mounting board, available in many different shades and colours from art suppliers. You need a straight edge, which is a ruler without measurements with a rubber underside so it won't slip. You also need a cutting tool of some kind, (a Stanley Knife, a scalpel or a cutter specially made to cut bevelled edges available from art supply shops), a ruler, a pencil, and some old card or a surface you can cut onto, as the surface you are working on will get damaged.

Mounting board marks easily, so you need a clean and dust free working area. Wash your hands before you begin, and keep them clean throughout.

Assuming you will be making your frames later, your first decision is how wide a mount you want – that is, how wide a space the work needs between its outside edges and the frame. Your work may need a wide border around it, or you may want the frame to be nearer the work. You may want an equal border all round the work or you may want a larger border at the bottom than at the top. Take time to make these decisions as this will effect the look of the work.

Calculate the size of the window you want to cut. If your window mount is to overlap the edges of the work, allow at least an eighth of an inch all round, so the work can be securely attached to it. When you have decided on the dimensions of the window you will be able to calculate the dimensions of the outer edge of your mount. Take into account the size of the rebate of the frame; the outside dimensions of the mount will be exactly the same as those of the glass and hardboard to go into the frame.

Cut the mounting board to the size you require. Then measure where the corners of your window will be on the front of the board and make a tiny pencil dot at each corner. If you are right handed, place the first edge to be cut at the left hand side. Place your straight edge slightly to the left of the two dots at either end – so you can just see the dots. Start your cut a fraction of a centimetre above the top pencil mark, and resting along the straight edge, bring your cutting knife slowly and smoothly down to the bottom pencil dot, and just beyond.

Turn your card so the second side is now to the left and cut each side the same way. Making each cut edge slightly longer than your measurement ensures that they cross one another at each corner so you end up with a clean cut. Otherwise you might be left with a 'woolly corner' as you take the central piece of card away.

When you have cut the window, turn the mount over so you can attach the work to the back. You will need brown paper tape and water. Brown paper tape is cheap, and acid free, so it will not discolour your work. Place the work over the cut window and using a small piece of tape secure the longest sides first, by placing the piece of tape at the centre of each side. The tape should be at the same position on opposite sides, and you should stick the opposite sides down at the same time, making sure the work is tight and straight. Then stick the two shorter sides in the same way. Finally, tape the corners down. You will need to let the brown tape dry out, so carefully weight the work down so it dries flat.

If the work is to float inside the window mount, tape the work to the backing board by folding the tape and again weight the work down while it dries. Then place the window mount around the work.

Cutting a bevelled mount with a special cutter is more involved, but follows the same basic principles.

It is important for a work to be well mounted; this should enhance the work rather than detract from it. A well made mount will allow the viewer to experience the work at its best without being aware of the mount. You will save a considerable amount of money by mounting work yourself, but if you feel you are unable to achieve a professional result have them done by a professional framer. A framer may make individual mounts for you even if you are making your own frames.

Making your own frames
Whatever type of frames you choose to make, you will probably always need to combine them with glass or perspex and hardboard.

The advantages of glass over perspex are that it is cheap and doesn't scratch. Perspex on the other hand, is lighter and stronger (it won't break so easily), but it does scratch, so may not look good for so long, it is also twice as expensive as glass. Perspex is probably most useful when you are framing very large works.

Glass is highly reflective. If your work is predominantly dark you will find the reflections obscure the work, so you might consider using non-reflective glass. This tends to be less clear and more expensive, but it does cut down on reflections. For small works use 2mm glass. For larger works, say over three square feet, use 3mm glass. If in doubt ask the advice of the glazier.

If you are making a number of frames it is worthwhile learning how to cut your own glass to size. This cuts costs and is relatively easy to do. Glass cutters can be purchased at hardware shops, and most have instructions. If not, ask the shopkeeper. Practise on scraps of glass until you are confident. You can also cut hardboard to size yourself. Score the smooth side of the hardboard with a Stanley Knife. It can then be cleanly broken along your scored line. Alternatively you can have glass, perspex and hardboard cut to size quite easily, but make sure the measurements you supply are accurate.

A simple and cheap way to frame works on paper, especially large ones, is to attach the work to the wall and then secure a piece of glass onto the wall over it.

Another cheap alternative is to use glass, hardboard and clips. The work is sandwiched between the glass and the hardboard, and the whole thing held together by the clips. The work can also be window mounted and framed like this. Cut the hardboard to size first, then cut the glass to the size of the hardboard. This will ensure both are the same size. If you are using glass rather than perspex, it would be best to have the edges of the glass ground by the glazier so you, and anyone handling the work, will not be cut. A glazier may do this, even if you cut the glass yourself.

Clips can be bought from most picture frame suppliers, art supply shops and some do-it-yourself shops. When you purchase them, ask how to use them. With this method you also need to attach hanging hooks to the hardboard. There are hooks made specially for this type of frame and you should purchase them at the same time as the clips.

You may wish to make wooden frames for your work. These days there is a huge variety of framing available, and if you make the frames up yourself it can be very cheap. You need to allow plenty of time, especially if you are making a considerable number.

The most important piece of equipment you need is a mitre saw which ensures accurate corners. Without this your frames will not look professional. If you don't have one yourself but you intend doing a lot of framing, it may be worth investing in one. The cost may be a lot less than having your frames made by a framer. You might even consider sharing the cost with friends.

You also need four corner clamps, a hammer, wood glue, panel pins, sandpaper, wood-filler and you may need screws, a screwdriver and a hand drill.

You can buy framing in lengths which is then to be cut down to exactly the right size and with a 45° angle. A mitre saw does this accurately, and once your corners are properly cut the rest is fairly simple.

When you have your four sides cut to size, glue the mitred ends which are to be stuck together, and secure each corner in a clamp. The clamp holds the frame together while the glue is drying. It is important to make sure each corner is square, especially with larger works. To make sure, measure diagonally between opposite corners. The two measurements must be equal.

Leave the glue to dry for the recommended time, probably about two and a half hours. Wood glue is very strong once dry, but a sharp knock can break the glue joint, so some additional strengthener is needed. Smaller frames just need one or two small panel pins driven into each corner, gently, so as not to break the joint. Make sure you hammer the pin straight into the wood, any angle may mean the panel pin splits or shows through the wood.

With larger frames, you need to secure the corners with screws. Drill a screw hole into one of the two lengths of framing to be joined, at each corner. Do this after the 45° angle has been cut, but before you glue the corner. Then use a countersink drill bit so the head of the screw will not appear above the surface.

Once the corners are secured, screw heads can be camouflaged with filler and the frame sanded and finished. You can purchase a wide variety of wood stains, varnishes, paints and waxes to finish your frame. If you use a stain, you need to seal it with a coat of clear varnish. Some varnishes are tinted so you could use one of these instead; it depends on what kind of finish you require. Try a few tests on scraps of wood.

When your frame is ready, the glass and hardboard can be cut to fit it. Always finish the frame first. Don't cut the glass and hardboard to size and then try to make the frame to fit. This is extremely difficult unless you are very experienced. Once the frame is made, you or the glazier can cut the glass to the size of the frame. This ensures a perfect fit and makes allowances if your frame is not quite square or is slightly bigger or smaller than intended. Hardboard can then be cut to fit the rebate of the frame. Measure the rebate but make the hardboard fractionally smaller so it can slip in and out easily.

You then need to prepare a clean and dust free area in which to assemble your framed work. Take your frame and place it front down on your working surface; make sure it is free of dust, etc. Place the glass in the rebate and without placing too much pressure on the glass, clean it thoroughly. Make sure there is no dust, grease or finger marks on it. Methylated spirits and a soft cotton cloth is the best way to do this. Make sure the glass is absolutely dry before you go on to the next stage. Take your mounted drawing and check there are no marks or specks of dust on either the mount or the work then place it face down onto the glass. Place a sheet of acid free paper on top; this prevents the hardboard from discolouring the work. Finally, place the hardboard on top of this.

Take hold of the whole thing with a hand on each side and holding the hardboard in place, carefully lift the frame and check the front to see if any specks of dust etc have managed to slip inside. If it is quite clean replace the whole thing face down again. You can then secure the glass, work and hardboard with tiny panel pins or special framing pins (available from framing suppliers). Tap the pins into the side of the rebate so the glass, work and hardboard are held down firmly and don't move about. You can then tape all round the join where the hardboard meets the frame with brown paper tape. This helps prevent dust from entering and finishes the frame off neatly, as well as helping to secure everything in place.

Once you get the hang of making your own frames it is really very simple, and will save a great deal of expense. If you have any doubts about being able to assemble the whole thing, take apart an already framed picture, and you will see just how easy it is.

If you find it difficult to obtain the kind of framing you require, or you feel you would like to make very individual frames for your work, you can buy good quality wood from wood merchants or from wholesale framers, and have a rebate cut into it on a circular saw. A local wood merchant may do this for you, although you will have to pay for the service. You then have framing which you can use completely plain, or which you can carve into or finish yourself in some way.

Professionally made frames

If you feel you are unable to make frames yourself, you may decide to have them made professionally. This saves a great deal of time and should ensure a good result. If you decide on this ask other artists to recommend framers. Always use one who is used to framing artists' work and have a look at previous work. Discuss what you want and ask how much it will cost. Bear in mind that materials are cheap but labour is expensive, so if you are having a number of frames made to the same specifications, it will be cheaper per frame than having individual ones made.

Organise this well in advance. If you need a number of frames made, the framer may need several weeks notice and if you need a rush job done, you may be charged more. At the agreed time phone to see if the frames are ready before you go in to collect them. Take your time to check that everything is as you specified, and each is up to standard. If you are collecting a number of frames don't forget you may need transport.

Other alternatives

You can buy framing cut to the sizes you require. This is a relatively cheap way to frame works, as you supply most of the labour, but the most difficult part, cutting the corners, has been done for you. Metal framing cut to size is the easiest to assemble, and does look smart. However this may not be the type of finish you require, and metal frames mark easily and it is not easy to camouflage marks on metal.

You can also purchase ready-made sets of glass/perspex, hardboard and clips. These come in standard sizes, but save time if you need to frame work in a hurry. Sets can be obtained from larger art supply shops, and some framing suppliers.

Another idea, is to look in a large discount store, you may find cheap framed prints at little more than the cost of the materials used in making frames. These may look rather cheap, but can be done up with a little sanding and varnish, stain or paint. Before you buy, check they are reasonably well made and sturdy enough to do the job. Consider whether you can turn them into something suitable for your work, and that the sizes are correct for what you want to do.

Relief works

If you work in relief, or your work might be damaged by being sandwiched between glass and hardboard, you will need to adjust your framing accordingly. You can purchase ready-made perspex box frames especially made for this type of work. These can be bought at some large art supply shops and framing specialists. However, they are expensive.

If you are making your own frames anyway, it is relatively easy to modify them to allow more room for the work inside. You can do this during the assembly of the framed work.

You need to choose framing which has a deep rebate and you need to purchase narrow strips of wood called beading. The size of the beading will be determined by the width of the rebate (that is the amount the framing overlaps the work) and the distance you need between the glass and the work. The beading is cut to fit into the rebate along all four sides of the frame, and is placed against the frame, between the glass and the work. You can fix the beading to the frame with a few tiny panel pins. You need to use a small tack hammer and tap the pins in very gently so as not to crack the glass.

Alternatively you may wish to make frames which are part of the work itself, especially if you work in deep relief. In this case you need to consider the frame along side the making of the work. You can usually use the simple procedures explained here and modify them to your own needs.

Framing works on canvas

Works on canvas don't generally require the same degree of protection as works on paper, but framing can enhance the presentation.

There are several simple ways of doing this. You can just paint or tape the edge of the canvas, or you can make a simple surround with thin pieces of timber fixed to the canvas with long panel pins. The use of a mitre saw ensures accurate 45° angles at the corners and helps to make a neat finish to the frame. Consider the depth of the wood. Do you want a frame the same depth as the canvas or deeper?

You may prefer a gap between the canvas and the frame. In this case you need to attach thin strips of timber to the canvas first, and then choose a wider frame which is attached on top of the smaller strips of timber.

You may feel you would like a fancier frame with a moulding. Framing can be purchased with rebates deep enough to accommodate the depth of a canvas. If you can't find what you want, have your own framing made on a circular saw as described above.

Finally, remember your framing needs to stand up to transport, hanging and visitors. So make sure your frames are well made, secure and won't damage the work they are intended to protect.

Your work may not require framing or it may not be possible to frame it, if for example, you make very large works on paper. If this is the case, make sure your work is well secured to the wall, and strengthened if necessary. Consider the situation in which the work will be hung – will it stand up to the situation and duration of your exhibition?

9 • Security & insurance

Security

Your exhibition will be open to the public and hopefully many people will see your work. However much you may want to trust people, and hope they are careful, there is always the danger of work getting damaged or stolen. So, well before your exhibition, think about the security of the place where you will be showing and the security of the work itself.

Find out how many access points there are and make sure locks on doors and windows are secure. Find out who locks up at night, if it is not you check the place will be secure and make sure you know who has access and who has spare sets of keys.

If the space has neighbours, get to know them. Tell them who you are, what you are doing and for how long.

If you are not required to invigilate the work, find out who will be there during opening hours. Is the person concerned in a position to oversee your work, or will they have other responsibilities which might take their attention away? Find out if your work will be within someone's vision continuously.

If you are responsible for invigilating, you need to arrange to cover all the opening hours of the exhibition, so consider this in advance. Remember you may well be spending considerable time in the space, so be prepared with plenty to do while you are there. If you are exhibiting with others, it is a good idea to try to divide each day. Remember you need to take breaks for lunch etc, so arrange for someone to cover for you.

Try to position yourself so all your works are in view, unless they are impossible to remove or damage. If some of your audience are young people or children, they may distract you, so be on your guard whenever someone is in the exhibition space. Don't leave purses, bags or belongings where you can't see them. Most people are trustworthy and there to look at the work, but guard against the few who are not.

Finally, never leave your exhibition unattended where the public are able to just walk in. If you have any doubts about the way your work will be overseen, think about how you can secure it, especially if it is small and light enough to be removed. If it can be screwed to the wall or floor, or secured in some way, you don't need to worry so much. If this is not possible you will need to find another way of securing it. This depends on the nature of the work, what kind of surface it is attached to and how it is attached.

Many small works can be attached to one another with thin wire, or something similar, which is either colourless or the same colour as the surface the work is attached to, so it can be discreet. Or you might find a way of tying the work to something else or to the nail, or picture rail or whatever it is hung on. With small pieces of sculpture, or equipment such as projectors you need to find some way of attaching them to the surface they rest on.

When you are hanging the exhibition, particularly when placing sculpture or equipment, make sure they are positioned so that people won't knock into them. Think particularly about the possibility of loss or damage during the private view when there may be a lot of people in the space at the same time. It is difficult to watch over the work in this situation, and people may be less likely to notice the position of a particular piece of work. It is also more difficult for visitors to look at the work at a crowded private view, so you might consider, particularly with sculpture, of rearranging things for it.

Insurance

Insurance of the gallery or space

Even if you take precautions against the possibility of damage or theft, these things can still happen. Insuring against these eventualities at least helps to compensate for any loss or damage.

Insurance of the space itself should include cover against fire, perils and accidents, etc. Most venues or owners of property will have insurance for the premises. But you need to know if the existing insurance is sufficient, and of the correct type for the use of the building as an exhibition space. Extra security or repairs might be necessary for a different use of a space.

Insurance of works

If you are exhibiting in a space normally used for that purpose, or in a venue where other activities are going on, you can usually assume that the building itself is insured against fire and other perils. But you need to check what insurance cover exists, if any, for work on the premises and if there is, whether it is adequate. If the space is insured but not for art works, try asking if insuring your work can be arranged for the duration of your exhibition; this may be possible to do in conjunction with an existing policy.

If insurance is your responsibility you may choose not to bother if you feel it is not worth the expense. If the venue is very secure and there will always be someone in attendance, it may be a small risk on the other hand you may decide it is worth paying for peace of mind, particularly if you are showing with other people, and sharing the cost. Cover should be against theft, fire and special perils, this will normally include malicious damage; it may be more difficult to get cover for accidental damage. You should always insure for the full value of your work.

Putting a value on your work for insurance purposes can be difficult. If you are already selling work regularly, your work has a market value; if you have never sold any work, how do you value it? You should insure for the price at which you would sell the work (see the section on pricing work). If you are selling the work unframed you need to include the cost of the frame on top of your selling price for insurance purposes.

An insurance company may dispute the value of your work and some might only be prepared to cover you for the materials used in the work and the framing. Of course, the work's value to the artist is much greater than just materials, so find an insurance company which is prepared to cover the value you put on your work. If you have sold work before at comparable prices to those you are putting on your work for the exhibition, this can help in persuading the insurance company that they are worth their selling price.

If you already have an insurance policy of some kind, for example house contents, your insurance company may be able to 'tag on' cover for your work during an exhibition. If you don't have any insurance try phoning round a few companies and see what the reaction is to your requirements. Alternatively, you may decide to approach an insurance broker for advice to find the right company and the right policy for you. Ask around other artists or galleries who may know a 'friendly' broker with experience in insuring art works.

Before you approach a company or broker, make sure you have all the details about the exhibition and the work. The company will need to know the period of time you need the work insured, so don't forget to include the hanging days, exhibition hours of opening, details of security and invigilation, the number of works involved, and their total value. You may need to provide a list of actual works, and satisfy the company the venue is secure, that someone will be in attendance and that the place is water-tight and has adequate fire precautions.

The number of works and their value will probably be an estimate at this stage, but bear in mind the greater the sum you insure for, the greater the premium (ie the sum you pay the insurance company). On the other hand, if you under insure, and you have to make a claim, you will only be paid a proportion of the value of the work lost or damaged. You should ask your broker or company about this before you complete the policy form.

You may also consider insuring your work in transit, for the period of time you are transporting work from the studio to the exhibition space, and back again. You should be able to do this in conjunction with insuring the work for the duration of the exhibition. Whatever you decide, take the advice of an expert and shop around for prices before you make your final decision.

Public liability insurance

You have made sure the space itself is insured and have insured your works against loss or damage. But what happens if someone trips over your sculpture and injures themselves? They may be able to claim against you or the owner of the building. Cover for this is called 'public liability' insurance. If the building is already used by the public for its original purpose, it will be probably be insured, as venues must be covered for this type of accident if members of the public are to be allowed in. The sum insured is usually very high, but the premium is low.

If the venue is not insured for public liability, you can make visiting 'by invitation only', so visitors enter the premises at their own risk. This should be stated on your printed publicity material. You still want to allow members of the public to enter, so place a prominent notice at the door stating entry is by invitation only and supply an invitation card to everyone who visits. If you do this you don't need to have public liability insurance but even if you make these arrangements, you may still be liable if you haven't taken proper care to see the space and the work are see 17 • Further reading of no danger to visitors. If you want more details on different types of insurance see AN Publications 'Fact Pack 6: Insurance'.

10 • Transporting work

Make the arrangements for transporting your work at least two weeks before you intend hanging the exhibition.

The method of transport depends upon its size, weight, the number of works, how fragile they are and the distance.

Transport

Your own transport

If you have your own transport, or a friend with a car or van big enough, this is probably the easiest and cheapest way. If a friend is moving work for you, make sure arrangements and details are fixed well in advance – be sure they are reliable and will arrive on time - you don't want to waste half your hanging time waiting for work to arrive.

Public transport

Public transport is a cheap alternative if your work is small and light. But think how many trips you may have to make. Check routes and times and find out if you need to change buses or trains, before deciding to use this method. Think about how much you are able to carry and remember, what seems like a reasonable weight to carry at first, will almost certainly seem much heavier by the time you reach your destination. If you have to make several trips, you may end up wasting time, and perhaps not saving money.

Taxi

If you are taking work a fairly short distance, and it will all go into a taxi, this can be a good and relatively cheap way to transport it and, being, 'door to door' will save time and energy.

Hiring a van and driver

Hiring a van and driver is probably the most expensive, but in the long run it can save time and trouble. If work is heavy, large or awkward this may be your only alternative. Phone around for a few estimates. If possible find a firm which specialises in handling art. Other artists who may be able to recommend specialist van hire firms, look in Yellow Pages, local service directories, and advertisements in specialist arts press.

When you phone up for an estimate, tell the firm what you are moving, roughly how many works, where your starting point and destination are, and how long you think it will take (loading and unloading will probably take longer than you think, so take this into account). Ask if there are any other costs over and above the hourly rate, eg a mileage charge, and if they make a minimum charge. Some firms will charge, for example, a minimum of four hours even if your job only takes one hour. Part of an hour will probably be charged as one hour, so check this too. Ask if the price includes VAT.

Hiring a self-drive van

If you can drive yourself, you can hire a van without a driver. This can work out cheaper if you are going long distances, but many firms charge by the day, so you may be better off hiring a van with a driver by the hour. Also remember you may need someone to help with the loading and unloading.

If you decide to hire a van, book at least two weeks in advance. During the exhibition, arrange for transport back again and don't leave this too late. If you are hiring a van it is a good idea to arrange your trip back on the day you take the work to the space, so you don't forget.

If you make oil paintings, or work in any other medium which needs time to dry or set, make sure it is finished in time before you have to move it to your exhibition space. If you have to transport work that is not dry, or indeed, work that is very vulnerable, it will have to be loaded extra carefully. This not only puts your work at risk, but also takes extra time loading and unloading, so adding to your costs.

Finally never hurry while transporting work, and if you are driving, drive carefully. A few minutes saved by hurrying will cost you if you have to repair work or framing.

Packing

How you pack your work will depend upon how fragile it is, how it is to be transported and whether you or someone else will be transporting it. The distance it has to travel doesn't make any difference, whether it is one mile or a hundred miles. If you are transporting the work yourself you may feel less packing is necessary, as you will be in control of its safety.

If someone else is transporting your work, pack every piece as well as possible. Be prepared for the fact that your work may be treated roughly.

Framed work with glass

Work framed with glass is particularly vulnerable, especially if it is large. Glass does not stand up well to stress. In case the glass does break, it is a good idea to place strips of masking tape across the front of the glass, from top to bottom and from side to side, at intervals of a couple of inches. If you use good quality tape it will peel off easily without leaving marks. This is a precaution; if the glass breaks it won't move and damage your work. If work is packed well this shouldn't happen.

Always protect the corners with pads of corrugated card, or if you don't have card, you can use newspaper, although this can mark a light coloured frame.

If you use perspex instead of glass, you won't need to tape the front as it does not break easily, but it is easily scratched, so cover the front of the work.

When loading your van or car, stack works on their edges, rather than flat, one on top of the other. If a work slips it can so easily apply pressure to work underneath. If weight is put on the glass part of a framed work, it is likely to break.

If you find you have to place works flat and on top of each other, make sure pressure is not put on the glass - wood should rest against wood. If you are loading several works of different sizes place two pieces of 2"x1" wood between each work and wedge everything in place so nothing can move.

Place some kind of packing between each work. Blankets are best, but you can use anything which absorbs vibration - like newspaper or card.

When you load the vehicle, tie and wedge everything in so nothing can move during transit.

Works on canvas

As with any two dimensional works, protect the corners with padding of some kind, then cover the whole thing with polythene; this protects and keeps the work clean. Make sure there are no projections which could damage another work.

When loading the vehicle, never lean anything on the canvas as it dents easily, prolonged pressure can leave a dent which is difficult to remove, and it could cause the paint to crack. Most dents in canvas can be removed by soaking the back of the canvas with water. When it dries out the canvas will have shrunk back into place.

When loading many canvases one beside the other, make sure frame rests against frame. If you are loading canvasses onto a roof rack, the same applies. If size makes this impossible, use strips of 2"x1" timber to separate one work from another. Rest the strips of timber in a position against the wood of both works it separates, and tie the timber down firmly so it won't move during transit.

If your paintings are too large for your vehicle, you can remove them from the stretchers and roll them. Always roll paintings around something like a cardboard tube. Don't roll them too tightly and roll with the painting on the outside which should help avoid cracking. Cover the whole thing with polythene. You can re-stretch the work in the gallery.

Three-dimensional works

It is difficult to advise on packing three-dimensional work as the variety is so great. You need to work out the best way for your own work – but use plenty of packing. One of the better methods is to use tri-wall cardboard boxes which are, in effect, a triple layer of corrugated cardboard. These can be custom-made to whatever size you want. The material is light and absorbs most shocks and is fairly resistant to penetration by sharp points. The one disadvantage is that it must be protected from water or damp which quickly diminishes its strength.

A variety of fillings can be used to absorb shocks and vibrations – wood-wool, chip-foam, polystyrene pellets and shredded paper. For touring wood-wool, chip-foam and polystyrene are best, though foam and polystyrene are not environmentally friendly. Shredded and crumpled paper disintegrates after a few handlings and will often need to be replaced or topped-up on a tour.

Very fragile and small objects should be double-packed – each item surrounded by filling in its own small container and a number of these packed again surrounded by filling in a larger tri-wall box.

For large three-dimensional work, bubble pack – a polythene sheet with a grid of air pockets is a useful material. If large works are being transported by someone else, you may need to pack them in crates.

When loading, tie and wedge work well so nothing can move, and no piece of work can damage any other.

In conclusion, always keep all your packing material, both for the return journey and for later use, as it can be expensive.

11 • Hanging the exhibition

Having spent so much time and energy making your work, it is important to present it to its very best advantage. Hanging your exhibition should not be rushed; allow more time than you think you need and be well prepared.

Preparation

A week or so before you start hanging have another look at the space. Note what kind of walls and/or floor it has and look at how the present show, if any, is hung. See how many power points are available, and where they are positioned; you may need an extension lead if the space is large or the power points are not conveniently placed. Have a look at the lighting. Is it adequate? Is it adjustable? You may have to attach the works to the walls in a particular way or there may be restrictions on what you can do. Think about how you will get your work into the space, especially if it is large, heavy or awkwardly shaped, or the space has difficult access and take measurements of the doorways and staircases.

At the same time, double check on when you can deliver your work, when you can have access and if there are any restrictions on the hours you can work in the space. Will you hold keys or will someone else have to open and close the space?

Check out the nearest hardware shop and stationer's, in case you need anything during hanging. It is also handy to know where you can get something to eat and drink.

Make a list of things you need for hanging, and put together a tool kit in good time. It saves time if you have everything to hand, instead of having to go in search of something during the hanging.

Below is a suggested checklist of things you might need. Add anything else you especially require and keep a list for future reference. Make sure you have plenty of screws, mirror plates, wall plugs, etc, which are all easily lost.

Checklist

- Hammer
- Screwdrivers (two or three sizes)
- Bradawl
- Electric drill (with percussion head for masonry)
- Drill bits for masonry and wood
- Staple gun
- Spirit level
- Pliers
- Tape measure
- Pencils
- Stanley knife
- Filling knife
- Extension lead
- Mirror plates (various sizes)
- Screws (various sizes)
- Masonry nails
- Wall plugs
- String
- Emulsion paint (for touching up)
- Paintbrush (for touching up)
- Polyfilla
- Sandpaper
- Vacuum cleaner
- Floor brush
- Dustpan and brush
- Blutack or similar (for labelling, notices)
- Stepladder
- Cleaning cloths
- Lint-free dusters
- Methylated spirits

Hanging

see also17 • Further reading

The amount of time an exhibition takes to hang varies greatly. It depends more on the nature of the work than the size of the space; so for even the smallest space you may need to allow two days for hanging, if you can. It is important to take the time to get things right; a badly hung exhibition can make even the strongest work look less than its best. You may be surprised at how much time you need to put a show together well.

There are four main steps in hanging an exhibition: placing the work; physically hanging it; arranging the lighting (assuming it is adjustable); and finally, labelling and presentation.

It may take twice as long as you think to hang your work. There are lots of little things which can hold you up, however much you plan in advance. Hanging a lot of small works takes much longer than placing a few large works. If your work is heavy or awkward this adds greatly to the time too.

Prepare a timetable, either in your head or on paper. This may seem difficult at first, but becomes easier each time you do it.

Your plan might go something like this: on the first morning decide on the placing of your work. Allow plenty of time, it is a very important part of putting together a good exhibition. During the second half of the day prepare your work for hanging, for example, attach mirror plates if you've not already done so. If your work is ready to hang, take a break, then come back to look afresh at your placing; there will still be time to make changes. Begin hanging work towards the end of the first day. Finish hanging by the middle of the second day at the latest, especially if your private view is that evening. Spend the rest of the day on presentation, and try to fit in a break before the guests begin to arrive.

You may want, or have to, hang your work in one day. This can easily be done with some kinds of work, but be prepared for a very long day. As you get tired you will begin to make mistakes and things will take longer as the day goes on.

If you are showing alone, arrange for at least one friend to help you. If your work is large or awkward you may need two helpers.

Placing your work is best done on your own or perhaps with one other whose judgement you trust, it may be helpful to have a second opinion at some stage. It is not a good idea to have more than three people putting together a show, unless it is a large event. If you have too many people hanging, too much time can be taken up making decisions but offers of technical or physical help are always useful.

Finally, always take along more work than you think you will need. This gives you extra choice when considering the balance and overall feel of your exhibition. You may be surprised at how different your work looks when you get it into the space, so you may end up making quite different decisions and with a very different show than the one you originally had in mind.

If you are involved in a group event, this may have to be arranged differently. Each artist will want to have some say in how his or her work looks. Discuss as a group, how this can be managed – you may decide to choose one or two people to organise the placing, with everyone else agreeing to accept their decisions. You might find a different solution, but try to come to an arrangement that is both practical and which satisfies most people involved.

Placing your work

Everyone has different ideas about how they want an exhibition to look. It is helpful to have looked at how others have hung exhibitions before doing your own – practise asking yourself what you think of the hanging of other's shows. You will find you learn from experience how to present your work to advantage and how to get the best from a space.

While trying to keep some basic rules or ideas in mind, try to approach placing your work with an open mind, allowing the whole thing to develop as you go along, being receptive to how things look and prepared to experiment.

Some spaces have very definite characteristics; dominant features or divisions that may help to suggest a start. The nature of the space in relation to your work may dictate certain arrangements. For example because of its dimensions, a piece of work can only go in one place and you then build the exhibition around this. In other spaces virtually any work can be placed anywhere.

Take your time in deciding where to place each work, move things around, trying different combinations until you feel quite happy with the position and look of each piece and with the overall show. Sometimes the two might seem incompatible, so try to achieve a good balance between the whole and the individual works. For example, you may have a favourite piece which just doesn't seem to work anywhere – try leaving it out. You may want visitors to see all your works, but not at the risk of ruining the overall impression and response.

Make sure you feel each work has enough space. Your exhibition may work best sparsely hung, or may look better hung closely. You can place works with fairly even spaces between them, or you may feel irregular spacing is more suitable.

Don't necessarily try to hang too many similar works with the idea that this will give a consolidated look to your exhibition; it could also look repetitive. Bear in mind that what seems to you, the artist, to be a considerable change from one work to another, may seem like hardly any change at all to the onlooker.

Resist temptation to show only the work you have made in the last few months. To you, your most recent work may be of the greatest interest and relevance; this will not necessarily be the case with your audience who may have seen nothing by you before. Most people will be interested to see the development of your work. Also, you may not be able to be so objective about work recently completed. It may be worth not exhibiting works you have still to come to terms with.

One of the primary aims of an exhibition is to interest people enough for them to look further, and for your work to remain in their minds. Give your audience plenty to get their teeth into. If their interest is sustained, they are much more likely to visit future shows.

Two-dimensional work

In deciding to hang one picture beside another, keep in mind that you want the placing to be interesting; don't necessarily go for a line of works of the same dimensions, although this may work well if the images relate to one another, or conversely, if they are very different. To create an interesting sequence, try an upright work next to a horizontal one. Consider how the composition of each relates to those beside it. A certain picture may not work at all at the end of a row of works, but it may look fine in the middle, and so on.

Colour is important too. What is the dominant colour in a work? How does it relate to those beside it? Too many bright or 'hot' coloured works may cancel one another out. Too many low key works may need a burst of colour.

The wall surface itself may affect the look, for example, a highly textured surface will detract from some works more than others. If the wall surface is different in different parts of the space, this may affect your decisions.

Large works will probably need to be seen from a distance. Small, delicate or intimate works may need to be seen from close up. Take this into account. Walk around as you think a visitor might and ask yourself where someone would stand to look at each piece.

In a mixed show, if there is perhaps only one work by each artist, the works are sometimes hung alternatively small and large. This can be effective in this type of situation, but this won't necessarily work well in a one or two person show. This may not work well in a mixed show either, you may decide to group two or three works of a similar size. While avoiding too much repetition, it will be important that works relate to one another in some way to avoid a bitty look to the exhibition. Consider how the scale of one work affects another beside it. Some may need something similar alongside to reinforce a statement; others may be better alone.

In a group exhibition where several works will be shown by each artist, it may work well to group one artist's work together, but on considering the whole show it might be more interesting to hang works by different artists together. Again, try several combinations before you decide.

Remember when placing work, and leaning them against the walls prior to hanging, they often appear to take up more space than when they are on the wall.

Three-dimensional work

The main and obvious difference between presenting two and three-dimensional work, is that three-dimensional work is usually seen from more than one angle, unless you arrange it otherwise. Similar decisions have to be made as with two-dimensional work, but from all view points.

Placing three-dimensional work can have one advantage over two-dimensional work, in that you can more easily move it around and see how it looks instantly as there is no lifting it into place on a wall, unless it is really heavy or awkward, or made 'in situ'. It is usually easier to make last minute changes, and of course there may not be any physical hanging. If this is the case, you may find you need less time than I've suggested.

However there are other things to be considered. Placing the work depends upon how, and from where, you want the viewer to see it. Ask yourself if the works need to be seen in relation to one another or as separate as possible. If the works must be seen separately you need more space for fewer works. Do you want viewers to walk in or around the works, or to view from the edge of the space? Do any works need to be seen against a white wall? Remember if you hang a drawing or other two-dimensional work on a nearby wall this will affect how the sculpture is seen.

Consider how each piece looks from all viewpoints, from close up and afar, and how all the pieces relate to any others within view at the same time.

If your works are placed on the floor, ask yourself how its colour and surface affects them. Bear in mind that the floor may not be flat or entirely horizontal, or it may be completely different from your studio floor. Does each piece need to be seen in a small, confined, or in some way delineated space, or does it need an expanse of space?

You need to consider the shape, form and colour of the works in relation to one another. Try to avoid too much repetition – make the whole exhibition an interesting combination.

It is difficult to be more specific, and you may find little of this relevant to your work. But I hope this has helped you begin to make decisions. Placing work becomes easier with practice, and get into the habit of noticing how other exhibitions are put together, and how you feel about the way they look.

Finally, there are two general rules which may help. If your work is presented well, you should be able to concentrate on each individual piece without distraction from any other, while, at the same time, the whole exhibition should look attractive from a distance and from any general viewpoint.

The other rule that only others may be able to judge, because you may be too close to the process, is that if a show is presented well, you should be oblivious of how it has been arranged, and only conscious of the work itself.

Attaching two-dimensional works to the wall

Before you begin, have a table or special place to keep equipment. This saves time searching for things during hanging. Return everything to this place when not in use.

In general, works should be hung at eye level or just below, ie the centre of the work being approximately five feet off the ground. This is not always possible, since walls may not be high enough, or you may feel the work actually looks better hung lower or higher. The space itself may be a determining factor, or the effect you want to create may help you decide. But remember tall people naturally tend to hang works high, while shorter people hang them low. Try to think in terms of the average height of visitors.

If you are hanging a row of works of varying sizes, don't align the tops of the works. They look better if the centres of the works are in line on any one wall, and if possible, throughout the exhibition.

It is advisable to hang the largest works first, especially the size of the works varies a great deal. Large works may need to be hung rather low, and if you are placing much smaller works around large pieces you may not be able to align the centres. Once you have hung a large work, ask someone to hold up smaller works while you step back to assess the best height in relation to the larger work.

To finalise the positions of the works, first determine your centre height. Remember, this will be just below your eye level if you are of average height. Working on one wall at a time, make a faint level line along the wall at this height. Do not rely on the floor itself being level, but mark your centre height in the middle of the wall and, with the use of a spirit level, draw a faint line either side of this point right along the wall.

Next, place your works along the wall as accurately as possible. This enables you to mark the position of the outside edges of the two outside works on your centre line. To get equal spaces between all works on the wall, measure the distance between these two outside marks, and measure the width of each work. Now take the total of the widths of the works from the length of the line between the two outside marks. Divide this measurement by the number of gaps and this will give you the exact distance between each work.

You can now work along your centre line from one end to the other, the centre point of each side of the work being placed on the line. Hang the first work at one end with its outside edge on the original outside mark you made. Then measure the gap you have already calculated, hang the next work and so on.

Mirror plates on the work are one of the easiest and most secure methods of attaching framed works and small canvases to a wall. Larger canvases on stretchers can be hung from the middle stretcher bar or from the top of the stretcher on two screws in the wall.

You have to make sure mirror plates themselves are placed exactly half-way down each side of your work if you intend hanging your work in the way described above. If they are not placed accurately, the works will not be level.

Most work can be hung with just two mirror plates (two plates will carry the weight of even a large drawing framed behind glass). You should only need to use more than two if the work is excessively heavy, or, if a painting is warped – the use of four plates will help flatten it to the wall.

To hang the work itself, line the edges with the marks made for it on your centre line with the centre line appearing in the hole of each mirror plate. Have someone hold the work so you can step back to make sure it is straight. You can use a spirit level to check, but having it level may not necessarily make it look level if the walls, floor or ceiling are themselves out of true. Rely upon your own eye for a final decision.

When you are satisfied it looks right, make pencil marks through the holes of the plates. Put the picture down, away from its position, as drilling will cause dust to fall. Drill two holes on the pencil marks, gently hammer in wall plugs if necessary, hold the work up and screw into the wall. Then proceed to the next picture.

The screws you use need not be any longer than three quarters of an inch. This size screw will hold quite a weight as screws are very strong, and there is no need to give yourself extra work by using long ones. But make sure that the drill bit you use, the wall plug and the screw are the same numbered size, so you have a good fit.

If you are hanging large canvases with horizontal cross pieces, you can use two large screws, screwed halfway into the wall, and half the width of the stretcher below your centre line. Then hang the central cross piece on the screws. If your stretchers don't have horizontal cross pieces, you can hang the top of the stretcher on two large screws in the same way. This system has the advantage that you can adjust the work laterally just by pushing the work along.

With small canvases it is advisable to use mirror plates, as they may be easily lifted off the wall and taken or damaged.

You will find the above procedure for hanging generally successful if you are careful, but it does take time. If you are very short of time it may be quicker to hang the whole show by eye. Simply have someone hold each work up and move it around until it looks right, mark your screw holes and screw to the wall. But you may not find it easy to do this well and accurately and for this, a spirit level is essential.

You may wish to hang your work in a less ordered way. For example you may choose to have varying spaces between the works, or you may not wish to hang it in a straight line at all. But however you choose, the same basic technical procedures apply.

When a whole wall is hung, step back and take a look. Are the works straight? Are the gaps the right width? How does the whole wall look? Small adjustments can still be made. Below are some tips for solving common problems.

see 'Quick tips', below

There are, of course, many other ways of attaching two-dimensional works to the wall. Mirror plates and screws are probably the most secure and accurate, but you may find you need to use another method. Your choice may be affected by the amount of time you have, the type of work you are hanging, the wall surface and the requirements of the venue.

A time saving alternative to using screws with mirror plates is to use masonry nails. This is also useful if the walls are very hard, but there are disadvantages. You won't be able to drive the nails all the way in, as they need to be removed with a claw hammer. When you remove the nails they are likely to make a mess of the walls, so there is extra patching up to do after.

Light work may be hung using ring eyes in the frame and nails or picture hooks in the wall. This causes minimum damage to the wall surface and the fixings are hidden from view. It is safer than using cord, but not as secure as using mirror plates.

You may decide to hang your work on one screw or masonry nail or picture hook, with the use of cord attached to the back of the work. This saves time, but it does also have is drawbacks. It is very difficult to hang a row of works accurately, the work can be more easily dislodged and it is more difficult to secure against theft.

If you decide to use this method with framed works, you will need to attach hanging rings to the hardboard before you assemble the frame. This ensures the work lies flat against the wall. If you attach hanging rings to the back of the frame itself, these will prevent the work from lying neatly against the wall.

If you are using cord of some kind, you need to make sure it holds the weight of the work. You can purchase special cord from frame makers, framing suppliers and some art supplies shops. This kind of cord, after being threaded through the rings can be twisted around itself. As strain is put on the cord, it tightens its grip.

If you use any other type of cord, for example, string, you will need to ensure it will take the weight and the knot does not slip. In this case use two or more separate strands of cord (depending on the weight of the work), so if one breaks the others still hold it.

The knot you tie should be a reef knot. A granny knot will slip if any strain is put on it; whereas a reef knot tightens.

Quick tips

There can be problems attaching two-dimensional works to walls, but in many cases there are simple solutions. Below are a few suggestions.

If it is a cavity wall, and only suitable for plugs and screws where there is battening behind the surface, you are bound to have to screw into the spaces between, which may just be plasterboard. There are special types of plugs available from hardware shops, which expand into the cavity to provide a rigid fixing. They are more expensive, but they work.

If you are hanging very heavy works on the cavity walls, these special plugs may not be adequate. If it is a partition wall and you have access to the other side, you can use butterfly screw fittings, also available from hardware shops. These are large bolts with a special nut which grips the wall behind. These will hold quite considerable weights.

A common problem when hanging two-dimensional work, is getting it to hang straight. Any amount of measuring may not ensure it looks straight or indeed is straight.

One reason why works may not look straight when hung, is because they are not square themselves. You can check whether this is the case by measuring the diagonals of the work; if the work is square they will be equal. If it is not square you will have to compromise between what the spirit level dictates and your own measurements.

If the work is square, there are ways of correcting slight slants caused by the hanging. One is to remove the screw holding the lower side of the work and pack the bottom of its hole with a matchstick or something similar, then replace the screw. This will also help if the screw won't tighten up, or if the hole is too large.

A work can be slightly adjusted by unscrewing both screws half way, and then tapping them with a hammer, one up and one down.

One cause of a slant can be that one of the screws has gone in crooked. You can check to see if this is the case by slightly unscrewing the screw. If it is crooked it will unscrew with a slightly rolling action to the head. The hole made by this screw will not be straight. You can leave the screw only half way in, this will slightly correct the slant, or, if need be, use a larger screw, but don't drive it all the way in. Camouflage with wall paint.

If you are still having problems with a canvas, especially a large one which would be time consuming to re-hang, you might try the following (but be careful): place a piece of 2" or 1" or similar timber on top of the canvas at the side that is too high; take a hammer and give it a sharp bang. This can slightly lower the work without you having to remove screws. Only try this with light, stretched canvases; it is highly dangerous to use on delicate or glazed works!!

Lighting

Lighting plays an important part in the way your work is presented, so put some thought into this. It may well be that the space has only general overhead lights, strip lights or conventional bulbs, in which case you may have to accept it as it is. It is possible to add temporary portable lighting available from lighting specialists, but this is likely to be costly. Most exhibition spaces will have adjustable lighting on tracks.

These will be one of two kinds – 'spots' or 'floods'. Spots are normally bulbs with built in reflectors that focus their beams on small concentrated areas. Flood lights, fitted with powerful tungsten halogen strips, give a very even spread of light over a wider area. The colour of the light from spotlights is normally towards yellow, whereas the colour from floods is generally colder, towards white.

Both types are normally fitted into tracks. This allows them not only to be moved along the tracks, but the fittings themselves allow for the lights to be swivelled and moved up and down.

Hopefully your exhibition space has good, even, reflected daylight. If there is direct sunlight you should screen this off because it may bleach the work and it gives different lighting effects as the day progresses. However, even if a space has good top light, this isn't necessarily enough to create an even light and you may need to add some artificial lighting.

Try to make sure the space is generally lit to a certain level with a combination of whatever is available. Daylight, fixed overhead lights such as fluorescent strips or conventional bulbs and flood lights. You can then use adjustable spots, if available, to make sure each work is sufficiently and evenly lit.

If daylight is available you need to set the lighting for both daylight and evening, especially in winter; your private view is likely to be in the evening.

Make sure all bulbs are working so you have the greatest possible choice of combinations. Check where to obtain spare bulbs in case they go during the exhibition.

There are some problems you might encounter with lighting. If your work is reflective you will lose detail if light is reflected from the work. This can happen with paintings and with works framed behind non-reflective glass. You may be able to adjust the light which is reflected - adjustable spots can be turned towards the ceiling to diffuse them. If this is not possible, try fixing a piece of paper or card in front of the light, but keep it well away from the bulb to ensure that it does not catch on fire.

When lighting three-dimensional works with spots, cast shadows may be a problem. The use of light and shadow may enhance a sculptural work, but remember each light directed at a work casts its own shadow. If you do not want shadows or direct light, diffuse the lighting in some way.

Try as many combinations as you can before settling for one which enhances each individual work and the whole exhibition.

Presentation

You have hung your work and adjusted the lighting, but there are still a number of things to do before the exhibition can open to the public. The final details of presentation are very important; if they are ignored they can let your exhibition down. If you pay attention to these details, your work will be shown to its best, so allow sufficient time for this finalising of your exhibition.

First there are finishing touches to be carried out to the works themselves. Dust them, especially if you have been using a drill. Make sure frames are clean. Touch up the edges of any unframed canvases. Paint mirror plates with wall paint so they blend in with the wall colour. Methylated spirits is best for cleaning glass and removing any grease or fingerprints on framed works. There are special solvents for cleaning perspex.

Clean up the walls and floor.

Most marks can be washed off the walls. If there is any touching-up to do, make sure the paint you use is the same as on the walls. There are many different colour 'white' emulsions and different finishes as well, and if you use the wrong paint all your touching-up may show. If there is any filling of holes to do, allow time for the filler to dry, then sand the wall surface smooth and touch-up.

Finally, look at the floor and any fittings which may need cleaning.

It is amazing how attention to details can give a real 'lift' to your work. Work shown in a clean and fresh environment will stand more chance of a sympathetic response. A cluttered or dirty environment will reflect badly on the work itself.

Information about the work

It is important to provide some information about the work to help make it more accessible and answer questions people may have. There are a number of ways to do this.

see 'Press release', 8 • Publicity

You can place labels on the walls next to the work, provide a price list for people to pick up as they enter, and provide information about yourself – a curriculum vitae and a short statement about your work.

You can vary the amount of information about your work between the wall labels and the price list or handsheet. One way is to simply number the works on the walls, these numbers referring to the information on the handsheet. Alternatively, you can put all the information on the wall labels except the price, which is then repeated on the price list/handsheet.

Whatever method you choose, keep it consistent. The information you usually want to give on the price list/handsheet (and/or labels) is the number of the work, title, date, medium, size and price. Indicate as a footnote what the size refers to, for example 'inches, height before width'.

If there is more than one artist you need to distinguish one artist's work from another. Either add the artist's name to the label by each work or, if each artist's work is grouped altogether you can place the name separately at both ends of the group of works.

You can buy sheets of numbers from stationers which 'transfer' straight onto walls or use sticky labels with numbers on them. If you want to give more information, type this onto sticky labels which can be stuck onto the walls. If the walls are not smooth, these labels can be placed onto card first, and although this is more time-consuming looks better. The positioning of labels relative to the work needs to be consistent.

Make sure the price list/handsheet is carefully typed and laid out. Have copies of this for visitors to pick up, so they can refer to it as they walk around. Make it clear on the handsheet that works are for sale. People are often reluctant to ask questions, so this information can be a great help.

If you have photographs of your work, it can be useful to have a few available. If someone from the media does visit, an attractive photograph of your work, or you and your work, might just help persuade them to include something about your exhibition, especially if they have a last minute space available.

Information about you, the artist(s)

It is interesting for visitors to have some background information on you. If you are not having a printed catalogue, have your curriculum vitae typed and copied. This can be available for visitors to pick up as they enter the exhibition. This helps give visitors a bit of history, and put your work in a context – especially important for those who don't know you.

You may decide to write a statement about your work to accompany your CV. If you have written a press release you could use this, or write something additional. Keep it brief and straightforward; think about who your audience might be, and whether or not they will already have an interest and experience of contemporary art. This depends on the type of space you are showing in, where it is located and who you have invited.

It might be useful to have a photograph of yourself somewhere, on the wall or with your information. This helps identify you if people you don't know want to talk to you.

A well laid out table or shelf for your information and a visitors book is a good idea. Leave some invitation cards here too, for people to take to remember you by.

Visitors book

Have a visitors book, even if it is only an exercise book ruled up with columns for names and addresses and the date. Encourage visitors to sign and leave their name and address, have the book at the entrance to encourage people to 'sign in'. If someone shows an interest in your work, add them to your mailing list for the future. You never know when a casual visitor may become a supporter of your work in some way.

All these extras help give your audience a context in which to see your work. It can encourage people to see you, and what you do, as approachable, and to take time and care over viewing your work. It may also help you sell work. Being able to communicate with your visitors is an important element in showing and selling.

Outside the space

Make sure the space, specifically your exhibition is well signposted from the street, particularly if the exhibition area doesn't open onto it, and make sure directions are clear if it is not easy to find. The gallery needs to look open and welcoming. Some people don't even realise they can just walk into a gallery, and some feel intimidated. They may also think they have to pay. A sign saying 'All visitors welcome', or 'Admission free' might be useful.

Access for the disabled

You may want to think about this. These days, some publications code places and events according to whether or not this kind of access exists. If it is easily done, for example by providing a ramp at the front door, you may encourage a few extra visitors. If your exhibition space does not look directly onto the street, consider the path which the disabled would have to take from the street to the exhibition and try to find ways to aleviate any problems they might have.

12 • The private view

This is normally the opening celebration: a chance for friends, potential purchasers, the press and others who may take a professional interest in your work, to see your exhibition before it opens to the general public.

If the exhibition is only on for a short period you may get more people along to the private view than during the rest of the time, so it is a very important part of the exhibition. It also provides a useful focus for selling work, and there may be more sales at the private view than later; the sense of occasion and celebration often encourages people to buy.

Since a successful private view is a good social occasion, there may be so many people it is difficult to see the work. It is certainly easier to concentrate on looking at work in an empty gallery. But if the work is interesting and well presented this will communicate itself through the general atmosphere.

If you decide to hold the private view soon after the hanging is completed, allow enough time to finish the work properly and to allow yourself to recover rather than feeling rushed or still putting finishing touches to the show as guests start arriving.

Arrangements

Planning for the private view should begin at least a week ahead. Decide what refreshments to provide; wine, beer, soft drinks, snacks. This depends on how many people you expect to turn up, what you can afford, and whether you charge for drinks. You need to make arrangements for ordering the drink, borrowing or hiring glasses and preparing any snacks.

Wine
Wine is a traditional and popular choice for private views. You can buy it by the case at wholesalers or wine merchants; one case contains twelve bottles, each holding approximately five and a half glasses. Wine

merchants and wholesalers can be found in the Yellow Pages or local directories. Phone around and compare prices for their cheaper ranges – it isn't generally worth considering more expensive wines for this type of occasion. French wines are usually best if you are going for the cheap wines, but most merchants will allow you to taste before you decide, if you are buying by the case. Try a few, especially if you intend charging for the wine. Normally it is best to buy half red and half white, except in summer when more white will be drunk.

Wine merchants should be able to supply you with glasses, usually free of charge. You may have to leave a cheque for their full value, which is either returned to you or torn up when you return the glasses. You have to pay for breakages, so before using the glasses check to see they are all there, or you may find you have to pay for more than you break. Some off-licences and wine merchants will buy back unused bottles, possibly at a small charge, if you enquire first.

Supermarkets can also be good places to buy cheap wines. You may be able to buy wine by the case here as well, but your may not get a discount for buying in bulk. Off licences are worth checking out, sometimes they have reasonable wines on offer. But supermarkets and off licences don't allow you to taste the wines, and supermarkets won't supply glasses. Off licences may have glasses available.

If your private view is in the summer and you are serving predominantly white wine, you need to chill it. A good relationship with your local publican may mean he will supply you with ice for the occasion. If so, try to arrange to collect the ice at least an hour before your guests are due to arrive. Remember to pick it up during the pub's opening hours which vary considerably these days. If this means several hours beforehand, it is still worth doing.

When you get the ice to the gallery (plastic bags will do to carry it), place it in a large bucket or some other suitable container and cover with cold water, the ice gradually melts into the water which goes on cooling the wine for hours.

Beer

If you decide to have beer, it is best bought by the barrel from a brewery or off licence. You should be able to purchase a good beer at a cheap price, but you will have to order in advance and pick it up yourself. In addition, live beer will have to stand in order to clear, for anything up to sixteen hours. You should not move it again after this, so you need to place it where it will be served. If these things present problems for you, try supermarkets or off licences, which may have a particular brand on offer. Some wine merchants do a limited selection of canned beers, this is another option, and some pubs and off licences sell 'polypins', which are small plastic barrels.

When calculating how much beer you need, allow for a certain amount of wastage with barrelled beer; you have to draw off the first couple of pints and you will probably have to leave some beer in the bottom of the barrel.

Glasses for beer may be difficult; breweries won't supply them. If you are on good terms with the local publican, this might be a place to try, especially if you explain about the extra customers you will bring after your private view. If you are buying from a wine merchant they may be able to help. If you can't get hold of glasses, you can supply plastic or paper ones.

Have some soft drinks available, such as fruit juice and bottled water.

Food

It is also a nice idea to have some food. It is relatively cheap to provide a simple buffet, but it will take some time to prepare. If you decide to do this, try to provide something which suits the occasion. For example, if your work relates to a visit to Italy, you could provide a few Italian type snacks. If you feel you don't have time to prepare food, or you feel it's more suitable, just have a few bowls of things to nibble.

How many to cater for

Knowing how much beer and wine to buy can be difficult. If you are not going to charge for drinks, this probably depends on how much you can afford to spend. If you are going to make a charge it is worth trying to arrange to take wine on a 'sale or return' basis, so you take more than you can actually afford to pay for. Some wine merchants do this; of course this can't be done with a barrel of beer.

The number of people who turn up will depend on who you invited. If you know most of those invited, then a large proportion are likely to come. But if most of your invitations were to people who don't know you, it is likely to be a small proportion.

A rough guide might be to suppose that a third of those invited will come, and aim to provide this number of people with two drinks each; more of course will be drunk if you can afford it.

If you can't afford to pay for much drink, consider making a small charge, but check first with the gallery or venue if need be. It is illegal to sell drink from premises unless it has a licence, but there is a commonly used (although legally questionable) way to get round this problem – you can ask visitors to make donations. You need a sign on your drinks table asking for donations of, say, 40p per glass. This means you can't force anyone to pay, but most people are happy to pay a small amount rather than take only one drink.

Other points to think about

Make arrangements beforehand for one or more friends to serve at your private view, and arrange for others to take over later on if necessary. Don't try to serve drinks yourself, you need to be free to talk to your guests.

Have your drinks table set up about half an hour before guests are due to start arriving. Unless you have an especially nice looking table, cover it with some kind of washable cloth. If your cloth isn't washable, cover it with polythene or use disposable paper ones.

Set clean glasses out on the table, tops downwards, which will distinguish them from dirty ones later on. Open a few bottles of wine before your guests arrive; red wine needs to be opened to breathe. Keep a little ahead of things by always having a few bottles open, in case things get busy, but slow down towards the end of the evening.

Have a bowl of hot soapy water and tea-towels behind the table, in case you run out of clean glasses. It also helps cut down on clearing up time afterwards. Have some cloths and a broom or brush and dustpan handy in case of accidents and make sure toilets are well signposted.

Be prepared for a mess to be left after the private view, especially if you expect a lot of people. If possible, clean up that evening – get started a little before the end. You can begin fairly unobtrusively by collecting glasses. Sweep up, get rid of cigarette ends, collect glasses and wash up so the gallery won't smell of stale tobacco and left over drink next morning. If it is not possible to clear up that evening, make sure you arrive in time the following day before the exhibition opens to the public.

If you are entirely responsible for the organisation of the event, try to keep yourself fresh throughout the proceedings and don't drink too much, as visitors may want to talk to you about your work, some may be interested in buying, and you will always want to be aware of what is going on. If your private view is at the end of your hanging days, you will be tired so plan to have an half-hour break before guests arrive.

At the end of the evening, make sure you are the last to leave and, if it is your responsibility, lock up securely.

Think about what you are going to do afterwards. You might decide to go for a meal with a few close friends and those who helped out. Perhaps you would prefer to spend the rest of the evening in the local pub where you can be with a greater number of your guests, especially if there are some people you have not had time to speak to.

Inform the police about your event, explain its function and how long it is likely to go on. This is especially important if the venue is not normally used as an exhibition space and would not have numbers of people entering and leaving in the evening. Consider if there may be problems with parking.

You may find you sell work at your private view, so be prepared. Purchase sheets of red dots at stationers and have a receipt book or sale agreement available; see the section on selling work for advice in greater detail.

13 • Selling your work

There are a number of reasons for exhibiting your work; you want your work to be seen, you may hope for some critical reaction, the experience allows you to see your work in a different context. For some artists, for example those who work with performance or installation, the exhibition is part of making the work, and for many it is a chance to sell.

Your work is not just the product of the time you spent making it, it is also the result of many years of experience and experiment. For each work you exhibit there are probably many you have rejected. Your work is the result of professional practice, and perhaps even more important, each is an original and personal statement. The idea of selling might be difficult to come to terms with but it helps cover costs and it may help support you in the future. Someone who buys now may well purchase other works later on, and through them your work may be seen by other potential buyers.

The idea of selling your work might affect what you choose to show. There is a great deal of difference between selling a museum sized piece of work and a work which would hang on the wall in someone's home. Those most likely to buy large works would be galleries and museums for public collections and major private art collectors. Early in your career it is unlikely you would attract this type of buyer; you would be much more likely to sell smaller works, to friends, acquaintances or possibly the local council or other local public places.

Pricing

Putting a price on your work is not an easy task, and you will find people have widely differing views on how to go about it. The suggestions here are general guidelines rather than hard and fast rules, and there are see 17 • Further reading many things to take into account. Pricing is covered in some detail by AN Publications 'Artists Handbook 3: Money Matters'.

First of all think of who your audience, and therefore potential buyers, might be. What kind of prices might they be prepared to pay? Those looking for something attractive for their home will probably have a sum in mind, and their decision will be made according to the price of the work and its size. There will be others who are able to pay anything you ask, and some will value your work more if it is more highly priced. Those who have bought contemporary art before will be used to the kind of prices you might put on the work. They expect to pay for quality, originality and for the name, if your work has sold and/or been exhibited widely. Those who have not bought contemporary art before are likely to think your prices are high even if you consider them to be relatively low.

You are a professional, so, like any other, you must think of the time you put into the work and how much remuneration you consider reasonable. Take into account your training and length of practice, your overheads such as studio rent, material costs and the exhibition expenses (these need to be spread over all the works). On top of this add the cost of framing.

If the gallery or venue takes a commission on any sales, this also needs to be taken into account. You have to decide whether to simply add on the sum you will pay in commission, or you may decide just to adjust the price of the work so as not to price your work out of reach of potential buyers. Ask the gallery if the commission is taken from the total price you put on the work or whether the price of the framing can be excluded when assessing commission, this affects your pricing too.

Check whether the gallery is deducting its commission from the retail price or whether it is adding it on to the price you want for the work. A 33.3% commission of the retail price is the same as a 50% mark up on the price that you want for the work.

The pricing of prints is slightly different. Prints are generally produced as limited editions, each is numbered and you guarantee only to print the number stated plus certain artist's proofs. Because there are a number of the same print you would tend to price these lower than a one off.

If this is your first exhibition, you may feel you can sell your work at fairly low prices. This may help you sell, but raise your prices as you continue to show and sell your work. If you begin by selling your work at higher prices, this could cause you problems. You can't lower the price of your work once you have sold and comparable works need to be priced consistently. If a buyer finds you have sold a comparable work to someone else at a lower price after selling to him or her, this will antagonise the original buyer and may affect your reputation with other potential buyers.

Consider all the works in your exhibition. Decide which you might sell for the lowest price of, say £60, and which you feel is worth the highest price of, say £500, then set all other prices between the two. It is a good idea to have a range of prices if you expect your audience to have differing views on what they can afford. Try to keep prices consistent with the quality of each individual work, and to a certain extent to the size.

It is not a good idea to say prices are negotiable. Most potential buyers like to have some idea of the prices, and time to consider their purchase before they approach you. Don't have too many of your works 'not for sale'. You may regret this later if several people express an interest in them, and you have sold nothing as a result. It also looks inconsistent with practising as a professional if you seem reluctant to sell. If you want to keep certain pieces, try to keep it to just one or two, or decide not to hang them. Have a sign up stating that works are for sale; not everyone assumes this.

Sales

Most of your sales are likely to happen during the private view, so be prepared. It is a tradition that red dots are placed beside sold works. (Although it has been known for dealers to put red dots beside unsold works to give an impression of the works' popularity and to encourage sales). You can purchase sheets of dots at stationers; keep them handy.

Have a receipt book. Some buyers will want one, and it is an easy way of keeping a record of where your work is, how much you sold it for and when. On the receipt include the title, medium and price, the date you sold it, the buyer's name and address, and sign it. Give a copy to the buyer and keep one yourself.

see 'Sales agreement', below If you prefer, you can draw up a sale agreement or have one drawn up for you, details are given below.

When you are selling work, take all the usual precautions as when selling anything. For example, ask to see a bankers card if you take a cheque.

If someone wants to reserve a picture without paying the full price right away, this can be difficult. Explain that unless they make a firm commitment you may have to sell to someone else. Take a percentage of the cost as a deposit, and explain this is non-returnable if they decide not to go ahead with the sale. You could use a different coloured dot beside the work, so others know this is not a definite sale if they are interested. (Have a key to explain this). This safeguards you when dealing with those you don't know. Of course it is different when dealing with friends or those who have bought before.

How do you encourage sales? You need to be able to communicate with people, talk enthusiastically about your work, and assess the person you are talking to as you go along. This may sound rather difficult, indeed, it is not easy for artists to sell their own work. Each situation is different, but if you persevere you learn by trial and error.

Some people will buy your work because they already know you and/or they are admirers of what you do, with these you probably don't need to make much effort to sell; if they can afford it they will probably buy. Selling work to others is more difficult, but there are a few tips.

When someone walks into your exhibition, watch how they behave, you will soon be able to tell whether they are interested in your work by how long they spend looking at it. You may see someone linger over a particular work, or go back several times to look at it. They may stop and discuss a piece with a companion. If someone does show interest, get into conversation with them. Start gently and generally, encouraging them to say how they feel about your work, listen seriously to what they have to say. You will soon be able to tell if they are thinking about owning something. If you can, try to help them to visualise your work in their home, if possible get them to visualise a particular spot where a piece might go. If someone seems genuinely interested but still hesitant to buy, try to establish whether it is the price putting them off. You may feel you can lower the price in one case, but try to do this quietly, or you'll find others want the same treatment. If you do reduce your price, remember if the gallery or venue is taking a commission, this may have to be paid on the listed price, not on the reduced price.

'If you are selling to members of the general public, of whom you have little knowledge, it is advisable that your terms of trade are that cash payment is made in full before you part with your work. Be warned that a cheque for a sum in excess of the cheque guarantee card limit scheme can be dishonoured by a bank, so it is not equivalent to cash. You are entitled to defer supply of your work until the cheque has cleared....

Be wary before providing anyone with credit. In essence this means that you part with your work before you receive your money. If for any reason they refuse to pay, it is often difficult to recover your work. You are therefore at risk and should only provide credit if you are fairly confident about the good reputation of the person.'
Deeks, Murphy & Nolan, 'Artists Handbooks 3: Money Matters'

You might offer to let someone pay in instalments, this can encourage new buyers, but be careful if you don't know the buyer well. Put the arrangement in writing, and if you are having to deal with the gallery or venue staff, you will need to discuss with them whether they can accommodate this type of arrangement. If commission is to be paid, sort this out before you finalise the agreement.

VAT

VAT on sale of art work is complex when a VAT registered gallery is charging commission on sales. The following information has been taken from AN Publications 'Artists Handbooks 3: Money Matters' which deals with VAT and the artist in detail.

see 17 • Further reading

'VAT can cause problems in the relationship between an artist and a gallery taking work on a sale or return basis, ie not buying the work in order to resell it.

If the artist is not VAT registered but the gallery is

- The gallery is entitled to add VAT to the sale price of your work because the general public will not be aware that you own it and not the gallery. As such the final sale price will be inclusive of VAT. This means that the net sales price on which a commission will be operated will be the sale price less the VAT.

- When charging you commission the gallery will be entitled to add VAT, ie if you have agreed a commission rate of, say, 25% then they can add on 17.5% VAT to this 25% making the charge in total 29.38%.

The way in which this works in practice is, for example, if you place a piece of work at a net selling price of £200 with a gallery and with an agreed commission rate of 25%:

- The price the customer will pay will be £200 plus VAT, ie £235

- The price on which commission should be charged is the net selling price, ie £200

- The commission that you will pay will be £50, but to this will be added VAT at 17.5%, ie £8.75, making a total commission payment of £58.75

- You will in effect receive from the gallery £200 less the commission plus VAT on the commission, ie £200 less £58.75, being £141.25

If both artist and the gallery are VAT registered

In this case you must also ensure that the transaction is properly recorded for VAT purposes in your own books. So, in addition to receiving notification from the gallery that the work is sold, and receiving a copy of their invoice for the commission (including VAT which you can reclaim from Customs & Excise), you must bill them for the value of the sale that has been passed on to the customer, ie you must raise an invoice for £200 plus VAT to the gallery which they can match up with the bill that they will effectively have to raise from them to the customer.

In this way VAT paid by the customer is effectively declared by you as your output VAT and the VAT charged to you by the gallery is declared as input VAT. Following the above example of a work with a net selling price of £200:

- The price the customer pays is £200 plus VAT, ie £235
- The price on which the commission is charged is the net selling price, ie £200
- The commission the artist pays the gallery is £50, but to this the gallery adds VAT @ 17.5%, ie £8.75, making a total payment of £141.25
- The amount the artist receives is not £141.25 as in the first example but £176.25, which is the difference between the gross selling price of £235 and the gross commission of £58.75. The artist receives the additional £35 because it is the responsibility of the artist to pay this to Customs & Excise rather than that of the gallery

Some galleries have what is termed a 'self billing' arrangement to make all this simpler, and this enables them to raise the bill from the artist to the gallery for the sale of a picture on your behalf. Many artists will find this convenient but it is essential to take advice either from Customs & Excise or an accountant before entering into such a scheme to ensure that the complications of it are understood. If you enter into a self billing arrangement and have given your written consent, you must never raise a bill to the other person in the arrangement but should accept that the information they provide to you constitutes your invoices and should be declared on your VAT return as recorded by them.'

Sales agreement

This could simply include the information above or some other conditions might be agreed. You may wish to put in writing your rights over the work, to include access to the work for future exhibitions, resale rights, copyright and the protection of the condition of the work. You might include the right of the buyer to resell the work and a guarantee the work will not deteriorate after sale. If you wish to draw up an agreement, and especially if you are in doubt about what to include and how to word it, you can consult a solicitor. Find one who has experience in doing work for artists or galleries. Ask around other artists or galleries for someone they can recommend. The following information has been taken from AN see 17 • Further reading Publications book, 'Making Ways' which gives a number of checklists for artist's contracts.

'Without a contract or agreement of sale the buyer is able, whether the artist likes it or not, to alter or damage (provided it is then not publicly exhibited or commercially published), or destroy the work, to prevent access to it including to the artist (for taking photographs for example), or to re-sell it to anyone else at any price. If you want to clarify any of these things put them down in a written sales agreement. British law provides little protection over the artist's work once it has been sold, except for copyright and the few moral rights provisions included in the 1988 copyright act. Under these provisions a work in which an artist has asserted his/her moral right of authorship may not be publicly exhibited or commercially published without sufficient acknowledgement of the artist. A sales agreement is a good place to assert this right of authorship. It is also worth clarifying the legal position that copyright is not transferred to the purchaser on the sale of the work, it belongs to the artist unless there is a written agreement to transfer copyright. Copyright and moral see 17 • Further reading rights are dealt in detail with in AN Publications 'Artists Handbooks 3: Copyright'.

Basic contract

- Name/address/tel of purchaser
- Name/address/tel of selling agent (if there is one)
- Name/address/tel of the artist
- Title, date and medium of the work
- Price paid or how payment is to be made and when.
- The artist retains copyright in the work.
- The artists asserts his/her moral right of authorship in the work in accordance with sections 77 and 78 of the 'Copyright, Designs and Patents Act 1988'.

Possible additional clauses

- The purchaser agrees to allow the artist reasonable access to the work for purpose of photography.
- The purchaser agrees to lend the work to the artist for purpose of public exhibition provided insurance and other defined conditions are met.
- The purchaser agrees to inform the artist if the work is resold or is given away and to whom, and when and where it is lent for exhibition.

- The artist agrees to repair damage to the work caused through faulty materials or craftsmanship (or if the work is inherently of an unstable or fragile nature then this fact should be drawn to the attention of the purchaser and any responsibility for repair disclaimed.

- The purchaser agrees not to intentionally to alter, damage or destroy the work.

- The purchaser agrees to inform the artist of loss or damage to the work and to give the artist reasonable opportunity to repair or supervise the repairs to the work.

- In using reproductions of the work the purchaser is restricted to the permitted acts as defined in sections 28-76 of the 'Copyright, Designs and Patents Act 1988'. Intended uses of reproductions for all other purposes must only be carried out with the prior agreement of the artist (copyright owner).

- Both parties agree to inform each other of changes of address.

14 • During your exhibition

General hints

Keep the space clean and tidy throughout the exhibition. Check every morning before you open up, that labels are intact and no work has slipped or been damaged.

If the exhibition is entirely your responsibility and you are going to be around most of the time invigilating, you will have a lot of time on your hands. But, there are ways you can use the time to actively encourage visitors and develop communication with your audience; you can learn a lot about your work through others' reactions to it. All this can be very valuable.

Written information about yourself and your work which you provide is the first step to communicating with your audience, so make this accessible to as much of your audience as you can. Not all visitors will have a knowledge of contemporary art, some will be interested, but find it difficult to understand what you are doing; others may be sufficiently interested to want to know more. Some may want to be kept informed about your future exhibitions.

Be friendly and encourage visitors to take part in the exhibition. This creates a good atmosphere, helps people to remember you and your work, and feel they have had an enjoyable, interesting and informative experience. Hopefully it will encourage interest, and if they have little experience of contemporary art, it might encourage them to see other shows; you may even encourage sales.

Listen to what people have to say; you can learn a lot. This is a time when you can think about how your work will develop in the future, and you can gain valuable information to help with your next exhibition. For example, ask your visitors how they heard about your show, this will help you learn how your publicity works.

Encourage everyone to sign the visitors book, make a special note of anyone who expressed a particular interest and add them to your mailing list. In this way you are constantly widening your audience and the possibility of selling.

If your exhibition is on for more than a week, and during the first week some people you had hoped might come haven't, give them a ring. They may just have forgotten, and even if they are busy, if you take the time to contact them, they might come along. You might even think of organising a small closing party at the end for people who couldn't come and to promote the possibility of sales. Use your invigilating time positively.

Education

Education, in the broadest sense, begins when you provide written information about your work, which helps make it more accessible. So think about who your audience will be and how you write about your work.

You may decide you want to do something more organised to extend your audience and their understanding. You may also wish to develop new skills and perhaps open up new opportunities for yourself.

There are a number of possibilities for using your exhibition to create more structured ways of informing and educating a wider audience. You need to begin to think about this, and plan any events well in advance, in time to advertise them through your exhibition publicity.

You might simply plan to give a talk about your work during the exhibition. This can be included in your publicity material and listings information, promoted locally in schools, colleges, community centres, galleries, local papers etc. You could contact the nearest college fine art department and find out if they would be interested in bringing a group of students along.

Giving a talk not only helps your audience to gain a greater understanding of your work and take more interest in what you are doing, it also helps you develop a very useful skill which increases your confidence, and possibly opens up new ways to supplement your income, it also gives you some insight into how an audience views your work.

You may decide to try to extend your contact with the local community, this can be approached in a number of ways. You could contact local schools and suggest setting up visits to your exhibition, and the possibility of holding workshops for school groups. You could approach local education centres, handicapped centres, youth clubs, community groups and hospitals and offer similar services.

If anyone expresses an interest, discuss what you might do, how this might be organised, what would be your responsibilities and how much they could contribute to the idea. If you are proposing workshops, ask if they can contribute materials.

When you have definite interest, you may need to seek financial help. Write a short statement about your intentions and a list of the interested groups. Then try approaching the local council and education authority for assistance. Even if they are unable to help you themselves, they may be able to suggest local trusts, or some other way of financing your proposed events, (see also the section on fund raising).

You may prefer to contact your local council or education authority first of all, rather than schools, etc, directly. Some will operate schemes for contact between artists and the community. Even if they don't, they may be able to suggest people who might be interested in working with you. There may also be galleries and other organisations which organise educational activities locally, so find out and contact them.

You may be able to think of other ways of attracting and informing those who might not otherwise visit your exhibition. What you decide to do, and how, will depend on a variety of things: the kind of work you do, how it can best be communicated; where and when you are showing; what other facilities, events, attractions and institutions are situated near your space, etc.

Whatever you decide, make sure arrangements and details are agreed and understood by both sides well in advance. If you are doing something more involved than an advertised talk, put in writing a brief description of the event, who is responsible for what, and include the place, date and times. You and the individual or group concerned should keep a copy.

If you are organising more than one event, or involving several groups of people, draw up a programme of events for yourself. Don't rely on yours, or anyone else's, memory. Double check that anyone supplying you with materials or equipment understands your requirements and has the correct dates and times. Establish who is responsible for the delivery and return of anything supplied by someone else.

If your event(s) is being financed by someone not directly involved, keep them informed and invite them to the event and your exhibition.

These events require extra planning and time, but they can be of enormous benefit. You may find it easier to raise funds to support your exhibition if you intend to encourage a wider audience, and you may find it easier to attract media attention; you will certainly find you have many more visitors, which makes you feel the whole experience has been of greater value. You may also sell more work, and/or find that such events lead to you being paid for some part of your work, either through being able to raise more funds or through payments from the existing budgets of the institutions with whom you work. You will undoubtedly find you learn a lot about your work through the reactions of others, and you will probably learn new skills and talents which in turn may well lead to new opportunities.

Finally, there is often no ready made audience for an artist's work and it is important to take responsibility for creating and expanding your own audience organising your own exhibition is an ideal opportunity to do this.

Documentation

If possible, take the opportunity to make a good photographic record of your work. Good slides and/or photographs have a wide variety of uses after your show. You may need to apply for exhibitions and other opportunities, or be asked to give a talk or lecture, you may need photographs for the press for future events, and you will want to keep a continuous record of your work. Also, if you sell work, you want a permanent record of it and it is useful to have a record of works which remain in storage and may not be accessible.

This is an ideal opportunity to photograph your work. It will be looking at its best, and will all be placed so it is much easier than having to set up work especially. So take advantage of the situation. It will, of course, be very difficult to photograph glazed work, so remember to document this before it is framed.

Your documentation will be of two kinds: firstly, a record of each individual work, and secondly, installation 'shots' showing how the exhibition itself looks. If you feel able to photograph it yourself this is obviously the cheapest way. If you don't have your own equipment you may be able to borrow or hire it. Find out from the local council or regional arts association what local resources exist. You might try contacting the nearest college fine art department, especially if you have had previous contact with them.

The equipment you need is a single lens reflex camera; a light meter (unless there is one built into the camera; in any case most photographers use a separate light meter), a tripod, and possibly photographic lights (if there is not enough daylight in your space). You may also need a wide angle lens.

If you feel unable to take your own photographs, try to find a friend with some experience to help you, or do the job for you. If they are able to help make sure they know what they are doing; try to see other photographs they have taken.

Employing a professional photographer is, of course, the most expensive way but you should end up with very good quality photographs and accurate colour. If you are not satisfied with the results in any way, you are entitled to have the job redone, at no extra charge.

If you are going to employ a professional, make sure he or she is used to photographing artists' work. Ask around other artists or galleries for someone they can recommend. Before you commit yourself, find out the hourly rate charged; material expenses will be charged on top. Describe what you need doing, what type of works and how many, and ask the photographer for some idea of how long the job might take. But allow for it taking longer, especially if your work, or the space, is unusual in some way.

The three most common ways of documenting work are: 35mm colour slides; 2¼" square colour transparencies (these are larger slides); and black and white prints. If you want colour prints, these can be made from slides, but you may lose some quality in the process.

35mm colour slides are the most usual form of documentation, they are useful for applications and for projection during slide talks or lectures. They are relatively cheap and it is a good idea to take perhaps five or six shots of each work.

2¼" square transparencies are more expensive, you need a special camera and you would probably need to employ a professional for this type of documentation. If you can afford it, 2¼" square transparencies have greater impact and in some situations help your work stand out among many applications.

If you are taking slides or transparencies yourself, the best way to achieve reliable colour is to use daylight film. If the space has some daylight, turn off all artificial lights even if the daylight is not very bright. If there is not quite enough daylight you will need to buy a 'faster' film. A fast film is one with a higher DIN (or ASA) rating, which will accommodate a lower level of light, and a lower reading on a light meter. Try taking a reading with a light meter to see if your normal film is adequate. If not, make a note of your readings and ask the advice of your photographic supplies shop if you are in doubt.

If your space does not have any daylight, you will have to use artificial light. Daylight films can still be used with some artificial lights, so it is worth taking a test film to see what the results are. You may find you need to use a tungsten film. For best results with this type of film you should preferably use photographic lights. If you have to use the existing artificial light, again, try taking a test film. If you are not happy with the colour, you can use special filters attached to the lens of your camera. You need to take the advice of your photographic supplies shop, as each case is likely to be different. You should be able to get advice as to which filter would help, but take your test film with you.

If you have any doubts about being able to make a good record of the work yourself, find someone who can do this for you; if necessary employ a professional. It is well worth having a good record; badly made slides will not do your work justice.

It is a good idea to have some black and white prints of your exhibition and at least some of the works individually. These are useful if you want to put together a press package in the future, they will be useful for some applications and can be used for other printed publicity material you might need.

You can take black and white prints in daylight, artificial light or a combination of the two, so there are less problems to contend with. It is more expensive to have prints produced than it is 35mm slides.

Whatever film you are using, colour slides or black and white, it is always worth taking each photograph with three different exposures, one either side of your meter reading. This will give you a choice of exposures and should ensure one good result each time.

Your documentation should be something you can feel confident about using after your exhibition is over. Good documentation can go on working for you over and over again, so it is worthwhile taking the time to see it is well produced.

see 17 • Further reading Photographing two- and three-dimensional work is covered in some detail in AN Publication's book 'Making Ways'.

15 • Final thoughts

There are no ready made, easy answers to the difficulties artists face. Some artists are more fortunate than others, but most have to create their own ways of dealing with the desire to make work, to have it seen, and the need to earn a living and feel part of the world around them. Artists are continually thrown back on their own resources and it becomes their responsibility to create a life and career for themselves. This can be difficult and frustrating, but it does give a tremendous amount of freedom in shaping your own life.

Organising your own exhibition involves a tremendous amount of hard work, initiative and perseverance; it can also be very rewarding.

It is important to realise that what you achieve will depend upon what you do and the approach you take. You need to have some idea of your goals, and how you intend to achieve them. At the same time it is important for your objectives to be realistic, both in terms of what you are likely to achieve and what you are actually able to do. It is important to see this experience as part of your life, as one step in your career as an artist.

At the same time, try to take a flexible attitude to what happens, and be constantly aware of how the experience of both the initial organisation and actually showing the work, can affect many other aspects of your working life. For example, learning to approach people and understanding their reactions to what you do can have huge benefits in quite different situations. Your achievements might actually turn out to be quite different from those you had first envisaged. Try to be open minded and prepared to learn as you go along, making the most of what arises, and building this experience into future plans.

You may have had quite specific aims; to attract media attention, to sell enough work to cover your costs, to be offered opportunities to show later on, to add to your reputation. These things are achievable; some more difficult than others and what you achieve may be different from the achievements of others, it is only by trial and error you discover what works for you.

However, you may achieve many things you are not even aware of at the time, but which will have benefits later. Someone who has seen your work may in future recommend you. If your publicity is good, your work will have been seen and/or your name remembered by many people, and you will not necessarily know who they are. You might find you realise other uses for the skills you have learnt, and that future opportunities are presented because of these new skills.

The exhibition you have organised is one element, but an important one, in the development of your career.

In these ways your exhibition can be used to enrich and expand your life and career as an artist.

You may feel despondent at not having achieved certain aims. Try to be objective; don't blame others. Use the experience to understand why you were not successful in these areas. Ask yourself how important they were and, if they remain important, how you could go on to achieve them. Hopefully the experience will give you some insight into problems, and perhaps suggest other ways of fulfilling these aims.

But look at the positive things you have gained. Ask yourself how they can be made to work for you in the future.

Opportunities for artists are continuously changing. New opportunities are created both by artists themselves and by the changing needs and views of our society. By widening your experience, skills and approaches to your audience, and by looking imaginatively at new ways of dealing with these changes, you can help yourself to make the most of situations and have more control over what happens to you. Use the experience of helping yourself, and organising your own exhibition, to take you forward in your career and open up new opportunities for you.

16 • Contacts

Arts and crafts councils

Arts Council of England, 14 Great Peters Street, London SW1P 3NQ, tel 0171 333 0100, fax 0171 973 6564.

Arts Council of Northern Ireland, 185 Stranmillis Road, Belfast BT9 5DU, tel 01232 381591, fax 01232 661715.

Arts Council of the Republic of Ireland/An Chomhairle Ealaion, 70 Merrion Square, Dublin 2, Republic of Ireland, tel [00 353] 1 661 1840, fax [00 353] 1 676 1302.

Arts Council of Wales/Cyngor Celfyddydau Cymru, Museum Place, Cardiff CF1 3NX, tel 01222 394711, fax 01222 221447.

Four regional offices: North Wales Office, tel 01248 353248; West Wales Office, tel 01267 234248; South East Wales Office, tel 01633 875389; North East Wales Office 01352 700236.

Crafts Council, 44a Pentonville Road, Islington, London N1 9HF, tel 071 278 7700, fax 0171 837 6891.

Scottish Arts Council, 12 Manor Place, Edinburgh EH3 7DO, tel 0131 243 6051, fax 0131 225 9833, email administrator.SAC@artsfb.org.uk

Regional arts boards

East Midlands Arts Board *(operates within Leicestershire, Nottinghamshire, Northamptonshire and Derbyshire except the High Peak District)*, Mountfields House, Epinal Way, Loughborough LE11 3HU, tel 01509 218292, fax 01509 262214, email ema@artsfb.org.uk

Eastern Arts Board *(operates within Bedfordshire, Cambridge, Essex, Hertfordshire, Lincolnshire, Norfolk and Suffolk)*, Cherry Hinton Hall, Cherry Hinton Road, Cambridge CB1 4DW, tel 01223 215355, fax 01223 248075.

London Arts Board *(operates within the Greater London area)*, Elme House, 133 Long Acre, London WC2E 9AF, tel 0171 240 1313, fax 0171 240 4578.

North West Arts Board *(operates within Cheshire, Greater Manchester, Lancashire, Merseyside and the High Peak area of Derbyshire)*, Manchester House, 22 Bridge Street, Manchester M3 3AB, tel 0161 834 6644, fax 0161 834 6969, email nwarts-info@mcr1.poptel.org.uk

Northern Arts Board *(operates within Cleveland, Cumbria, Durham, Northumberland and Tyne & Wear)*, 9-10 Osborne Terrace, Jesmond, Newcastle upon Tyne NE2 1NZ, tel 0191 281 6334, fax 0191 281 3276, email norab.demon.co.uk

South East Arts Board *(operates within Kent, Surrey and East and West Sussex, excluding Greater London)*, 10 Mount Ephraim, Tunbridge Wells TN4 8AS, tel 01892 515210, fax 01892 549383, email sea@artsfb.org.uk

South West Arts Board *(operates within Avon, Cornwall, Devon and Dorset, except Bournemouth, Christchurch and Poole, Gloucestershire and Somerset)*, Bradninch Place, Gandy Street, Exeter EX4 3LS, tel 01392 218188, fax 01392 413554, email swarts@swarts.zynet.co.uk

Southern Arts Board *(operates within Berkshire, Buckinghamshire, Hampshire, Isle of Wight, Oxfordshire, Wiltshire, and the Poole, Bournemouth and Christhurch areas of Dorset)*, 13 St Clements Street, Winchester SO23 9UQ, tel 01962 855099, fax 01962 861186, email sarts/info@goe2.poptel.org.uk

West Midlands Arts Board *(operates within Hereford & Worcester, Shropshire, Staffordshire, Warwickshire and West Midlands)*, 82 Granville Street, Birmingham B1 2LH, tel 0121 631 3121, fax 0121 643 7239, email west.midarts@midnet.com

Yorkshire and Humberside Arts Board *(operates within Humberside and North, South and West Yorkshire)*, 21 Bond Street, Dewsbury WF13 1AX, tel 01924 455555, fax 01924 466522, email yharts-info@geo2.poptel.org.uk

Printers and transport firms

Inclusion in the following lists is in no way a recommendation or stamp of approval by the author or AN Publications and has been compiled from organisations who have advertised their services in Artists Newsletter.

Specialist postcard printers

Abacus (Colour Printers) Ltd, Lowick, Near Ulverston, Cumbria LA12 8DX, tel 01229 885361, fax 01229 885348.

Just Postcards, 136 Lauriston Road, Victoria Park, London E9 7LH, tel 0181 533 4000.

Loudmouth Postcards, The Workstation, 15 Paternoster Row, Sheffield S1 2BX, tel 0114 275 3175.

Transport firms

Shuttle Services, Malvern House, 28 Grosvenor Place, Jesmond, Newcastle upon Tyne NE2 2RE, tel 0191 281 1397, fax 0191 281 6734, mobile 0831 854518.

Dragon Security Services, 6 Joiners Road, Linton, Cambridge, tel 01223 893805, mobile 0585 060276.

AWD, 4 Cleavedale, Downend, Bristol BS1, tel/fax 0117 957 0158, mobile 0836 627520.

17 • Further reading

Many of the books and articles in the exhibiting section contain general information on all aspects of exhibiting such as finding and approaching galleries, publicity, transport, insurance, security, etc. It is also worthwhile consulting your regional arts board or arts council to see what advice and information they can offer.

At the end of this list there are several smaller lists looking at particular subjects.

Books and Fact packs published by AN Publications can be ordered using the form at the end of this book or by credit card on 0191 514 3600. Photocopied articles from *Artists Newsletter* are available at 50p a page.

Exhibiting - general

Artists Newsletter Essentials. AN Publications, Available free to subscribers. Contains listings of national press and media contacts, business support agencies, information resources, and much more. With extensive further reading list. Available from AN Publications.

A Code of Practice for the Visual Arts, Lee Corner/NAA. Aims to establish principles which will assist artists and those with whom they work, to arrive at mutually beneficial arrangements. Available from The National Artists Association, 1995, Spitalfields, 21 Steward Street, London E1 6AJ, tel 0171 426 0911.

Running a Workshop: basic business for craftspeople, Barclay Price, 3rd ed 1995, ISBN 0 903798 80 8, £7.50. Aimed at craftspeople, looks at exhibiting, selling, costing, premises, exporting and other general topics. Available from the Crafts Council, 44a Pentonville Road, London N1 9BY, tel 0171 278 7700.

'Studios practice', Dinah Clark, *Artists Newsletter*, November 1996, pp17-18. Organising an open studio event can be an effective way of exhibiting work. Organisers and artists discuss strategies. Available from AN Publications.

Seeing the Light, Rhonda Wilson (ed), 1993, ISBN 0 905488 19 9, £10. Includes information on self-promotion, copyright, finances, and much more. Available from Nottingham Trent University, Bonington Building, Dryden Street, Nottingham NG1 4EU.

Exhibition spaces

Directory of Exhibition Spaces, Janet Ross (ed), AN Publications, 4th ed, 1995, ISBN 0 907730 27 2, £14.95. Lists over 2,000 exhibition spaces throughout the UK and Republic of Ireland. Describes art forms shown, exhibition policy and gallery space.

Arts Review Yearbook 1996/97, Arts Review Magazine,1996, ISBN 0 904831 26 4, £9.95. Includes a listing of galleries throughout the UK. Available from Hereford House, 23/24 Smithfield Street, London EC1A 9LB, tel 0171 236 4880, fax 0171 236 4881.

Investigating Galleries: the artist's guide to exhibiting, Debbie Duffin, 1994 (with updated bibliography), ISBN 0 907730 22 1, £9.95. Full of information to improve an artist's or maker's chances of exhibiting, and minimise rejection and discouragement. With advice of how to approach galleries, present work and deal with commision on sales.

The Guide to Exhibition Venues in Ireland, Sarah Finlay (ed), 1995, ISBN 0-906627-60-5, £5.95. Features over 180 galleries and exhibition spaces in Ireland. Available from The Arts Council of Ireland, 70 Merrion Square, Dublin 2, Republic of Ireland, tel [00 353] 1 661 1840.

London Art and Artists Guide, Heather Wadell, 1997, ISBN 0-9520004-1-5, £9.95. List exhibition spaces throughout London, interviews with artists and art maps. Available from London Art and Artists Guide, 27 Holland Park Avenue, London W11 3RW, tel 0171 221 6983.

Publicity & promotion

Arts Council Press Contacts & Press Mailing Lists, Arts Council, 1996, £25. Two annually-updated listings, one of arts contacts in the press and media and the other of arts contacts throughout the UK arranged by artform and geographic region. Available from Press Office, 14 Great Peter Street, London, SW1P 3NQ, tel 0171 333 0100.

'Artful attraction' & 'Creative communcation', Jo Scott, *Artists Newsletter*, March & May 1995. Outlines the steps to take to ensure that your work gets noticed.

'CVs with savvy' & 'Vernacular spectaculars', David Briers, *Artists Newsletter*, June & July 1995. Outlines the dos and don'ts of the reumé and investigates the state of the statement.

'Catalogues of disaster (and how to avoid them)', Stephanie Brown, *Artists Newsletter*, April 1995. Takes a critical look at catalogues and offers advice to first-time catalogue producers.

'No cornflakes packets please!', Bridget Fraser, *Artists Newsletter*, April 1995. Step-by-step guide to putting together exhibition applications.

'Getting into print', Sharon Kivland, *Artists Newsletter,* December 1996. The author writes about her approach to self-produced catalogues and books, and provides a practical checklist for reference.

Fact Pack: Photographing works of art, Peter White. Covers two- and three-dimensional work, with advice on which materials and equipment to use. Available from AN Publications.

Essential Business Guide 96 & **Essential Marketing Guide 96**, Essential Strategies, £7.50 and £5.50. Offer advice on planning, budgeting, marketing, CV formats, useful addresses and much more. Available from Essential Strategies, 44 Parkhill Road, London NW3 2YP, tel/fax 0171 482 5397.

Transporting work & insurance

Fact Pack: Insurance, Philippa Levy, 1996, £1.85. Includes advice on arranging insurance for exhibitions. Available from AN Publications.

Exhibiting and Selling Abroad, Judith Staines, 1994, ISBN 0 907730 21 3, £9.95. Contains useful chapters on exporting your work, including packing, insurance and transportation. Available from AN Publications.

Legal issues

Introduction to Contracts, Nicholas Sharp, 1992, £3.50. Outlines the elements and terms you might find in a contract, and provides artists with the ammunition they need to negotiate, deal with disputes and find a suitable solicitor. Available from AN Publications.

NAA Public Exhibition Contract, National Artists Association/ Richard Padwick, 1993, £3.50. Covers the legal arrangements surrounding showing work in public galleries and exhibition spaces. Available from AN Publications.

Galleries, Dealers & Agents, Nicholas Sharp, 1996, £3.50. Includes three model contracts which look at costs, publicity, gallery commission, insurance and ownership, copyright and moral rights, long-term gallery representation and the agreement of the agent's and artist's obligations. Available from AN Publications.

Selling Contracts, Nicholas Sharp, 1993, £3.50. Looks at sale transactions and the legal consequences of a sale, setting out suggested forms of contract to ensure that the artists' position as seller (and usually copyright owner) is protected. Covers selling to private buyers, galleries and shops and includes ready-to-use contract forms for sale or return and direct sale. Available from AN Publications.

Fact Pack 6: Insurance Chris Mcreedy, AN Publications, 1991, £1.50. Includes advice on arranging insurance for exhibitions. Available by mail order only from AN Publications.

Insurance, Chris Mcreedy, *Artists Newsletter*, July 1991, p36. An introduction to insurance for artists. Available from AN Publications.

Legal issues

NAA Model Exhibition Contract. National Artists Association, 1990, £5. A sample exhibition contract designed specifically for use by artists and publicly funded galleries (in draft form). Available from NAA, 17 Shakespeare Terrace, Sunderland, SR2 7JG.

Artists Handbooks 4: Copyright, Roland Miller, AN Publications, 1991, ISBN 0 907730 12 4, £7.25. Includes advice on copyright and moral rights in exhibitions and promotional material.

Pricing your work

Fact Pack 1: Rates of Pay, Susan Jones, AN Publications, 1991, £1.50. Includes information on exhibition payment right and examples of rates of pay for exhibition commissions. Available by mail order only from AN Publications.

Artists Handbooks 3: Money Matters Sarah Deeks, Richard Murphy & Sally Nolan, AN Publications, 1991, ISBN 0 907730 11 6 £7.25 (inc p&p). Includes information on pricing your work, commission agreements with galleries and VAT.

Selling

'Selling from the studio', Oliver Bevan, *Artists Newsletter*, July 1989, p28. Although written from the angle of selling from a studio, the article includes useful advice for selling in any situation. Available from AN Publications.

'Selling in craft galleries' David Butler, *Artists Newsletter*, March 1990, p35. Three craftspeople talk about how they find spaces and outlets for their work. Available from AN Publications.

'Hanging Exhibitions', Oliver Bevan, *Artists Newsletter*, October 1991, p30-31. Advice on how to hang, arrange and present work in 2-D. Available from AN Publications.

18 • Index

19 • Advertisers' Index

Other AN Publications

AN Publications is the only publisher to specialise in information for visual artists, photographers, time-based artists and craftspeople. So if you need to know:

what awards, competitions and opportunities are in the offing
which galleries are worth approaching to show your work
how to make the most of your skills
who supplies 'green' art materials
where to find help, information and advice
when to apply for grants
and any other practical information, we can help you through our directories, handbooks, 'Fact Packs' and monthly magazine, *Artists Newsletter.*

Artists Newsletter	The essential monthly magazine packed with up-to-the-minute information on residencies, awards, commissions, jobs, competitions, etc. The visual artist's 'lifeline'.
Making Ways	*The visual artist's guide to surviving and thriving.* Written by artists for artists, with first-hand advice on all aspects 'business' practice. 368 pages.
Directory of Exhibition Spaces	A comprehensive listing of over 2000 exhibition spaces in the UK and Eire to help you find the ideal space for your work. 500 pages.
Residencies in Education:	*setting them up and making them work.* Explores the strengths and weaknesses of 6 residencies, to help you get the best out of placements of all kinds.124 pages.
Health & Safety:	*making art & avoiding dangers.* Advice on health and safety across all art and craft forms. Plus help on preparing COSHH assessments. 128 pages.
Money Matters:	*the artist's financial guide.* User-friendly advice on: tax, national insurance, keeping accounts, pricing work and much more. Features an accounting system devised for artists. 128 pages.
Copyright:	*protection, use & responsibilities.* Essential advice on negotiating copyright agreements, exploiting earning and promotional potential, and dealing with infringments. 128 pages.
Organising your Exhibition:	*the self help guide.* Excellent advice on all aspects of organising exhibitions, from dealing with printers to buying wine. 128 pages.

AN Publications, PO Box 23, Sunderland SR1 1BR. Tel 091 567 3589. Fax 091 564 1600

Across Europe:	*the artist's personal guide to opportunity and action.* Artist's first hand experiences in 20 European nations help you take your first steps into europe. 200 pages.
Live Art	Unique advice on putting a performance together, touring work, copyright, contracts, etc with lots of examples of live art. 192 pages.
Independent Photography Directory	Listing of over 250 organisations involved with photography plus awards, fellowships, funding bodies, press lists, etc. 224 pages.
Code of Practice for Independent Photography	Guidelines for successful negotiations with advice on employment, copyright, exhibiting, commissions... plus sample fees and rates of pay. 32 pages.
FACT PACKS	Indispensible factsheets for artists, makers and administrators.
Rates of Pay	Information on current pay rates for artists.
Slide Indexes	Includes a national listing of artists' registers and slide indexes.
Mailing the Press	Includes a press list of national dailies, weeklies, and magazines.
Getting TV & Radio Coverage	Includes a contact list of TV and radio stations.
Craft Fairs	Includes a selected list of national and international fairs with details.
Insurance	Advises on types of insurance artists need, and why.
Post-graduate courses	A detailed listing of post-graduate courses in the UK.
Green Art Materials	A listing of 'green' art products and suppliers.
New Technology for Artists	Includes a listing of supplier's, courses and hands-on facilities.
Basic Survival Facts	Essential practical information for all new artist's on getting started.
OTHER BOOKS	We also supply books produced by other publishers covering areas such as fundraising, crafts and illustration. Please ask for our brochure.

AN Publications, PO Box 23, Sunderland SR1 1BR. Tel 091 567 3589. Fax 091 564 1600

ORDER FORM

Only UK prices given, phone for overseas prices

		Qty	£
A Code of Practice for Photography	£3.25		
Across Europe	£9.95		
Copyright	£7.25		
Directory of Exhibition Spaces	£12.50		
Health & Safety	£7.25		
Independent Photography Directory	£5.00		
Live Art	£9.95		
Making Ways	£11.99		
Money Matters	£7.25		
Residencies in Education	£7.25		
Artists Newsletter	issue		
£15.00 UK individual, £25.00 UK institution			
Annual subscription beginning with ___			
Fact Pack 1: Rates of Pay	£1.50		
Fact Pack 2: Slide Indexes	£1.50		
Fact Pack 3: Mailing the Press	£1.50		
Fact Pack 4: Getting TV & Radio Coverage	£1.50		
Fact Pack 5 : Craft Fairs	£1.50		
Fact Pack 6: Insurance	£1.50		
Fact Pack 7: Post-graduate Courses	£1.50		
Fact Pack 8: Green Art Materials	£1.50		
Fact Pack 9: New Technology	£1.50		
Basic Survival Facts	£1.50		
	TOTAL		

Name/Address

Name

Address

Postcode   Telephone

Payment by cheque/postal order

Send cheque/postal order made payable to AN Publications

Return to: AN Publications, FREEPOST, PO Box 23, Sunderland SR1 1BR

Payment by credit card   NB Visa/MasterCard only

Card number

Expiry date

Return to: AN Publications, FREEPOST, PO Box 23, Sunderland SR1 1BR

Credit card telephone orders 091 514 3600 (Mon – Fri 9-5)

☐ Please send me a free sample issue of Artists Newsletter

AN Publications also distributes books for the visual arts produced by other publishers, ask for our full publication list.

If you found this book useful...

...help us stay in touch with your needs and interests by filling in and returning this freepost form. Your opinions are important, and will help us to continue to publish the kinds of books you need, when you need them. To thank you for your help, we will send you a discount voucher for use when purchasing other books from AN Publications.

Title of book _____

Where did you buy it? _____

Why did you choose it?
- ☐ Best coverage of the subject
- ☐ Recognised the author
- ☐ Recognised the publisher
- ☐ The price was right
- ☐ Other (please specify) _____

Where did you hear about this book?
- ☐ Book review in _____
- ☐ Leaflet in _____
- ☐ Advertisement in _____
- ☐ Browsing in _____bookshop
- ☐ Personal recommendation
- ☐ Other (please specify) _____

Have you any comments on the content of this book?

_____

_____

_____

_____

_____

Thank you for taking the time to fill in this form. Where shall we send your discount voucher?

Name _____

Address _____

_____ Postcode _____

SEND TO: Lynn Evans
AN Publications, Freepost, PO Box 23, Sunderland SR1 1BR

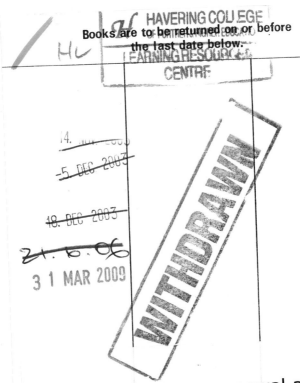
For enquiries or renewal at
Ardleigh Green LRC
Tel: 01708 455011 Ext.2040